South Carolina

Nature
Viewing
Guide

Author

Patricia L. Jerman

First published August 1998

Steering Committee

The following is a list of steering committee members who participated in Nature Viewing Guide site selection and production approval. Their support has been invaluable to this project.

Oscar Stewart, USDA Forest Service
Brock Conrad, SC Department of Natural Resources
Erskine Suber, SC Department of Transportation
Pete Spearman, SC Forestry Commission
Irvin Pitts, SC Department of Parks, Recreation & Tourism
Larry Davis, USDI Fish and Wildlife Service
Fran Rametta, USDI National Park Service
Dave Brady, US Army Corps of Engineers
Norman Brunswig, National Audubon Society
Bobby Harrell, SC Handicapped Sportsmen

Nature Viewing Guide cooperators include:

SC Department of Natural Resources,
PO Box 167, Columbia, SC 29202

SC Department of Parks, Recreation and Tourism,
1205 Pendleton St., Columbia, SC 29201

SC Department of Transportation,
PO Box 191, Columbia, SC 29202

SC Forestry Commission,
PO Box 21707, Columbia, SC 29221

SC Handicapped Sportsmen
7449 Hendersonville Hwy.
Yemassee, SC 29945

US Army Corps of Engineers,
4144 Russell Dam Drive, Elberton, GA 30635

USDA Forest Service,
4931 Broad River Road, Columbia, SC 29210

USDI Fish and Wildlife Service,
4801 Hwy. 17 N, Awendaw, SC 29429

USDI National Park Service,
200 Caroline Sims Road, Hopkins, SC 29209

National Audubon Society,
Francis Beidler Forest, 336 Sanctuary Road,
Harleyville, SC 29448

Contents

Front cover: *Raven Cliff Falls in Greenville County. See page 28.* Photo by Phillip Jones.
Back cover: *DonnelleyWildlife Management Area in the ACE Basin. See page 101.* Photos by Ted Borg.

3

Contents (continued)

Contents  (continued)

site *page*

Acknowledgements

The *South Carolina Nature Viewing Guide* captures the essence of the Palmetto State's natural heritage through a vibrant depiction of 93 places to see nature at its best. Author of the guide, Patricia L. Jerman, uses a conversational writing style to whisk sightseers away to breathtaking places that have inspired writers and artists from around the world.

As you journey through South Carolina, take time to savor the natural splendor of the state's dramatic mountain vistas, lush foothills, mesmerizing rivers, serene bottomlands and salty shores. These places harbor a magnificent array of plants and animals, historical sites and other significant features.

We hope you will enjoy visiting South Carolina's nature viewing areas and that your memories will be as vivid as the photographs in this book. To ensure these spectacular places will also be seen firsthand by future generations, please remember to collect litter and avoid disturbing the plants and animals that make these protected lands so special.

This guide was produced through a cooperative effort between the USDA Forest Service, SC Department of Natural Resources, SC Department of Transportation, SC Department of Parks, Recreation and Tourism, SC Forestry Commission, USDI Fish and Wildlife Service, USDI National Park Service, US Army Corps of Engineers, National Audubon Society and SC Handicapped Sportsmen. Information on the areas featured in the guide was contributed and approved by a host of biologists, site managers, educators and conservationists.

The following people assisted in the organization and production of South Carolina's Nature Viewing Guide. Many thanks go to:

- Kelly Russell of USDA Forest Service, for organizing the steering committee, coordinating site selections and getting South Carolina's Nature Viewing Program off the ground!
- Oscar Stewart and Barnie Gyant of USDA Forest Service, for guide coordination.
- Brock Conrad and Prescott S. Baines of SC Department of Natural Resources, for guide coordination.
- Erskine Suber of SC Department of Transportation, for sign and guide coordination.
- Brent Dillon of SC Department of Transportation, for directions and sign locations.
- Cindy Thompson of SC Department of Natural Resources, for guide coordination and editing.
- Glen Connelly of SC Department of Natural Resources, for technical advice and printing coordination.
- Ellen Fishburne Seats of SC Department of Natural Resources, for editing, layout and design.
- Linda Renshaw, Caroline Foster, Mike Creel, Greg Lucas and Beth Mason of SC Department of Natural Resources, for editing.
- Ted Borg of SC Department of Natural Resources, for photography and coordination of photograph selections.
- Mike Creel, Michael Foster, Glenn Gardner and Phillip Jones of SC Department of Natural Resources, for photography.
- Art Carter and Robert Clark, former DNR employees, for photography.

Introduction

South Carolinians have always been close to the land and its wild inhabitants. In Colonial times — when observing and understanding wildlife, weather and the rhythms of the growing season were essential to survival — no one called "nature viewing" a pastime. Now, however, it is an increasingly popular hobby.

Bald eagles (Haliaeetus leucocephalus) *have made a remarkable recovery in South Carolina. Once nearly eliminated, birds in our state now number more than a hundred nesting pairs. This juvenile is being shown a basic take-off maneuver.* Photos by Phillip Jones.

Despite the abundance of television shows, books and games that teach us about the natural world, there is no substitute for firsthand experience. There are also the benefits of beautiful scenery, exercise and spectacular photo opportunities. Most importantly, it teaches children the value of observation and questioning, and the need to take care of the habitat we share with many other creatures.

This guide was written to showcase superb spots for nature observation in South Carolina. More than 100 sites were nominated, and those selected had to meet strict criteria. Many magnificent sites could not be included due to space limitations, inaccessibility, or the need to protect fragile natural communities from damage.

Nature viewing areas featured in this guide include mountaintops, swamps, beaches and unusual geologic formations. Some are excellent bird-watching sites, while others are known for their spring displays of wildflowers. Some offer hunting or fishing opportunities; others shelter endangered animals or plants. All have something to teach us.

Enjoy your exploration of some of the best natural areas South Carolina has to offer. Remember that each of these areas, and the plants and animals that live there, deserve your respect and need your protection.

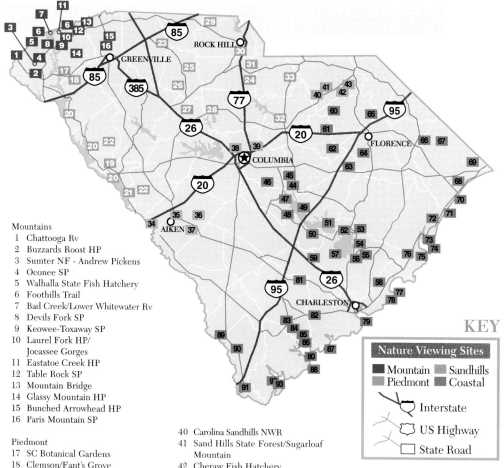

KEY

Nature Viewing Sites

■ Mountain ■ Sandhills
■ Piedmont ■ Coastal

⌂ Interstate

⌂ US Highway

☐ State Road

Mountains
1 Chattooga Rv
2 Buzzards Roost HP
3 Sumter NF - Andrew Pickens
4 Oconee SP
5 Walhalla State Fish Hatchery
6 Foothills Trail
7 Bad Creek/Lower Whitewater Rv
8 Devils Fork SP
9 Keowee-Toxaway SP
10 Laurel Fork HP/
   Jocassee Gorges
11 Eastatoe Creek HP
12 Table Rock SP
13 Mountain Bridge
14 Glassy Mountain HP
15 Bunched Arrowhead HP
16 Paris Mountain SP

Piedmont
17 SC Botanical Gardens
18 Clemson/Fant's Grove
19 John de la Howe
20 Savannah District Lakes
21 Stevens Creek HP
22 Sumter NF - Long Cane
23 Pacolet River HP
24, 25 Turkey Management -
   Chester & Union Counties
26 Rose Hill Plantation SP
27 Sumter NF - Enoree Ranger
28 Lake Monticello/Parr
   Reservoir/Broad Rv
29 Kings Mountain SP
30 Rock Hill Blackjacks HP
31 Landsford Canal SP
32 Lake Wateree Dam
33 Flat Creek HP/ Forty-Acre
   Rock

Sandhills
34 Savannah River Bluffs HP
35 Hitchcock Woods
36 Aiken SP
37 Aiken Gopher Tortoise HP
38 Harbison State Forest
39 Native Habitat Learning Center/
   Clemson Sandhill Research &
   Education Center

40 Carolina Sandhills NWR
41 Sand Hills State Forest/Sugarloaf
   Mountain
42 Cheraw Fish Hatchery
43 Cheraw SP

Coastal Plain
44 Poinsett SP
45 Manchester State Forest
46 Congaree Swamp
47 Upper Santee Swamp
48 Santee SP
49 Santee NWR
50 Santee Cooper WMA
51 Bird Island (Lake Marion)
52 Sandy Beach WMA
53 St. Stephen Fish Lift/Jack Bayless
   Hatchery
54 Lake Moultrie Passage/ Palmetto
   Trail
55 Wadboo Creek
56 Old Santee Canal SP
58 Francis Beidler Forest
59 Francis Marion NF
60 Kalmia Gardens/Segars-McKinnon HP
61 Lee SP
62 Lynchburg Savanna HP
63 Woods Bay SP
64 Lynches Scenic Rv
65 Great Pee Dee Rv HP
66 Little Pee Dee Rv HP

67 Cartwheel Bay HP
68 Lewis Ocean Bay HP
69 Waccamaw Rv HP
70 Myrtle Beach SP
71 Huntington Beach SP
72 Samworth WMA
73 Tom Yawkey Wildlife Center
74 Santee Coastal Reserve WMA
75 Santee Delta WMA
76 Hampton Plantation SP
77 Cape Romain NWR
78 Capers Island HP
79 Fort Johnson-Marine Center
80 The ACE Basin
81 Edisto Rv
82 Edisto Nature Trail
83 ACE Basin NWR
84 Donnelley WMA
85 Bear Island WMA
86 ACE Basin NERR
87 Edisto Beach SP
88 Hunting Island SP
89 Webb WMA
90 Tillman Sand Ridge HP/WMA
91 Savannah NWR
92 Victoria Bluff HP
93 Pinckney Island NWR

About South Carolina

A drive of only five hours will take you from broad sandy beaches, across tidal marshes and freshwater swamps, through agricultural fields and forests, over sandhills left by the Atlantic Ocean thousands of years ago, across the fall line, and into the piedmont and mountain regions of the state, with waterfalls and gorges to rival some found in national parks. Not surprisingly, these diverse landscapes host equally diverse plant and animal communities, providing a wealth of nature viewing opportunities.

South Carolina's **mountains** are part of the Blue Ridge Escarpment, stretching from Virginia to Georgia. The Escarpment is part of the Appalachian Mountains, which reach into Canada. An old mountain chain, the Blue Ridge's tallest peak in South Carolina, Sassafras Mountain, is only 3,554 feet above sea level. The Blue Ridge Mountains of South Carolina are located in Oconee, Pickens and Greenville counties, and make up only about two percent of the state's land mass.

High rainfall and abrupt changes in elevation make this an extremely interesting region, with spectacular waterfalls, many of which can only be reached on foot, and the largest concentration of endangered species in the state. A good way to see the mountains of South Carolina is to travel the Cherokee Foothills Scenic Highway (SC 11).

At the base of the mountains, South Carolina's **piedmont** region slopes toward the fall line. Remnants of its more mountainous past can still be seen at Glassy Mountain and Paris Mountain in Greenville County, but for the most part, the region is made up of modest hills and valleys.

Part of the state's history and adorning its flag, the palmetto tree is a proud native resident of South Carolina's coast.
Photo by Phillip Jones.

The **sandhills** mark the boundary between the piedmont and the coastal plain. This region consists of hilly sand ridges, many of which are ancient sand dunes formed nine to 12 million years ago. The sandhills can be very dry, yet they are home to interesting plants, found in few other locations. The sandhills are found in Aiken, Lexington, Richland, Kershaw and Chester- field counties.

The fall line marks the point at which rivers "fall" from the piedmont to the flatter coastal plain. Columbia, North Augusta and Camden were all built at the fall line, the uppermost point of navigability along the state's great rivers. These cities became commercial centers because of the shipping trade and the availability of water power for industries.

The largest geographic area in the state is the **coastal plain**, extending from the sandhills to the coast. Rivers in the coastal plain meander through extensive swamps and bottomland forests, carrying a heavy load of sediment with them. About 10 miles from the coast, freshwater swamps turn brackish, then salt. Rivers drop their loads of sediment, making the area a nutrient-rich nursery for the abundant life of estuary and open ocean. South Carolina has 183 miles of coastline, and some of the best preserved wetlands on the East Coast.

How to Use This Guide

Viewing areas featured in this book have been divided into four sections based on geographic regions of the state: Mountains, Piedmont, Sandhills and Coastal Plain. The general location of each viewing area is displayed on regional maps at the beginning of each section. Within each region, sites are grouped based on proximity to one another, making it easier to plan trips. Detailed directions are included in site descriptions.

Each site description includes the following information:

<u>Recreational icons:</u> Symbols that indicate facilities, such as restrooms, or opportunities, such as camping, that are available at that site.

parking area — restroom facilities — picnic areas — foot trails — interpretive centers — camping areas

small boats — large boats — boat ramp — access fee(s) — lodging on site

restaurant on site — bike trails — great for birders — great for children — great for botanists — wheelchair access°

° Note: Access may be limited. Some sites may be wheelchair-accessible but not noted as such in this publication. Please call ahead to each site you are visiting for detailed information.

<u>Description:</u> A general description of the area, highlighting the most interesting features.

<u>What to look for:</u> Types of animals, plants or habitats expected at the site.

<u>When to go:</u> Information about hours of operation as well as prime viewing times.

<u>How to get there:</u> Directions are given from the nearest town listed in the state highway map index.

<u>Extras:</u> Additional information, including phone number or other sources of information.

As you travel around South Carolina, look for these signs. They show the way to each of the nature viewing areas included in this guide.

Abbreviations used in this guide:

DNR	SC Department of Natural Resources
HP	Heritage Preserve
NF	National Forest
NWR	National Wildlife Refuge
PRT	SC Department of Parks, Recreation and Tourism
Rv	River
SP	State Park
WMA	Wildlife Management Area

Watching Wild Things

When you go to a zoo or other educational facility, wildlife has been "brought to you" for your enjoyment and education. When you go to one of the sites included in this guide, or to any other natural area, the tables are turned, and you become a guest in the home of the animals and plants you hope to observe. You enter their habitat. The less you disrupt the life of your "host" the more enjoyable your experience will be... as with a visit to a human habitat.

Here are some points to keep in mind on a nature viewing trip:

Avoid disturbing animals. Some animals could hurt you. Most could be hurt by you. Young animals that appear to be abandoned generally have a parent nearby. Remember that nature viewing practices, such as using artificial calls or banging on cavity trees, while not directly harmful to birds, may be disruptive, especially during the nesting season.

Photo by Michael Foster.

Plants need protection, too! A nature photographer who stands on top of three perfect flowers in order to take a picture of a fourth will make the next observer's experience far less enjoyable. Unlike animals, plants can't move out of your way. Use caution and try to stay on paths or trails if at all possible. Don't move vegetation from around a den or nest to make it easier to see. If it is easier for you to see, it will be easier for a predator to find. Don't dig up plants in the wild. Most don't transplant well, and it is often illegal.

Please don't feed the animals. Human food may harm wild animals, and it is illegal in some cases. Animals that get handouts of food lose their fear of humans and are more likely to be hurt by cars, dogs and careless individuals. Some animals are also more likely to hurt humans.

Clean up after yourself and others. Leave the area cleaner than you found it, and always carry trash bags with you. Litter left behind may still be there hundreds of years from now and may cause harm to countless plants and animals.

Stay on trails, boardwalks or other walkways. Minimize damage to the habitat. Some people think they can see more off the trail, but you make less noise on the trail. You will also be less likely to twist an ankle on uneven ground or get scratched by dense vegetation.

Photo by Michael Foster.

Viewing Hints

Use binoculars: Binoculars are almost a must. To choose binoculars suitable to the places and situations you expect to use them, refer to magnification and lens numbers. The first number refers to magnification level; the larger the number the closer objects appear. The second number refers to lens size; larger numbers indicate greater light-gathering ability and field of view. With 7x35 binoculars, (an all-purpose model) the object appears seven times closer than the human eye can see, and the diameter in millimeters of the front lens is 35. To increase magnification and light-gathering ability, you may choose from 7x50, 8x40, 10x50 and many other models. Serious nature-watchers may also invest in a higher magnification spotting scope and tripod.

Photo by Phillip Jones.

Take a camera: The best times to photograph wildlife are early morning or late afternoon, when animals are more active and when the light is softer. Know your subject and its habitat. Remember, don't let your desire for a good photo put you, your subject or its surroundings in danger. Beginning photographers should note that pictures in books and magazines may give a deceptive idea of how close the camera is to the subject. Many spectacular photographs are taken with powerful zoom lenses or in controlled situations such as zoos or parks. Like selecting binoculars, choose a camera and lens that will match the expected use. Ask experienced photographers for advice before investing in camera equipment.

Don't forget field guides: Field guides will help you identify plants, trees and wildlife that are native to the region you are visiting. Many guides also include information on animal markings, habits, behaviors and habitats. Consider guides that are compact, informative and easy to use.

Dress for comfort — and for safety: Before you depart, check weather reports and dress appropriately. Carry water, energy bars or fruit, sun block, protective eye-wear and rain gear at all times. A day-pack or backpack will conveniently carry these items, along with a field guide, camera, binoculars and other essentials. In the South, carry insect repellent during the spring, summer and fall. In cool or cold temperatures, dress in layers that may be peeled off if you become warm. To stay warm and dry, wear a nonabsorbent, wicking layer of underwear of polypropylene or similar synthetic, covered by layers of wool and, in rainy weather, an outer shell of waterproof rain gear. Rain gear should be donned before other clothes become wet. Comfortable, closed-toe shoes or hiking boots are usually recommended for nature viewing trips. Wear water-resistant shoes or boots in wet or swampy areas. It is a good idea to wear hats or vests of

international orange color to be easily seen during hunting season. Many public lands require you to wear international orange. Check the area's regulations to be sure.

Look in the right places: Understand the viewing area. Is it swampy or dry? Deeply forested or open? If you understand the characteristics of the viewing area, you'll have a better idea of what plants and animals you might expect to find there. Conversely, if you are looking for a particular animal species, go to places that are likely to have its preferred food, vegetative cover and nesting opportunities. Remember to avoid getting too close to wildlife — for your safety and theirs.

Look at the right time: Once again, understanding wildlife and wildlife habitat is essential. Most animals are more active in early morning or late afternoon, but some, like butterflies, may be more visible at midday. Many birds migrate through South Carolina in spring and fall; time your visits accordingly. And of course, be sure your destination won't have locked gates on the day of your visit!

Understand your subject: The more you learn about plants, animals and other natural resources, the more enriched your outdoor experience will be. Match calls and sounds to the animals making them. Study wildflowers, where they grow, and insects attracted to them. Or take note of the geology, soils and water that support the habitat.

Tag along with an expert: Take advantage of every opportunity to travel with an expert naturalist. He or she will know the best places to look and will know what to look and listen for.

Be aware of hunting seasons: Refer to "Rules & Regulations: Hunting, Fishing & Wildlife Management Areas in South Carolina" to avoid scheduling a nature viewing trip on public hunting lands during hunting season. For more information, you may contact the site manager or request hunting information from: SC Department of Natural Resources, PO Box 167, Columbia, SC 29202, (803) 734-3886.

What you can do to help:

If you are interested in protecting wildlife and natural areas, you can:

- Follow changes in the law: Support proposals to create new parks and refuges. Speak out against threats to existing natural areas. Make your voice heard. Look for ways to contribute to plant and wildlife restoration. One way is through the purchase of a SC endangered species license tag.
- Consider the needs of wildlife in your own back yard. Provide food, water, shelter and safe places to rear young. To certify your back yard as a Backyard Wildlife Habitat, contact the SC Wildlife Federation at (803) 771-4417 or the National Wildlife Federation at (800) 822-9919.
- Join a local land trust, or a state or national group dedicated to protecting natural areas and native species.
- Most important of all, teach your children and your friends' children about nature.

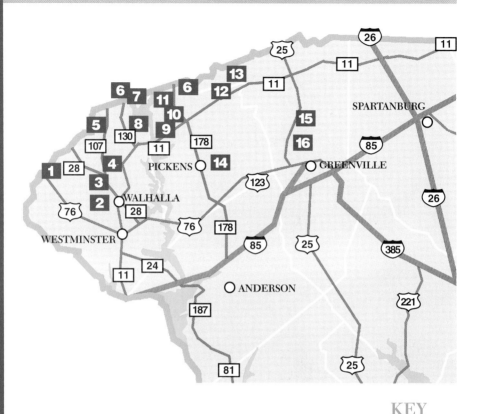

Mountains

KEY

Nature Viewing Sites

Mountain Sandhills
Piedmont Coastal

Interstate
US Highway
State Road

14

Whether you ride the rapids, fish for trout, or simply admire its beauty, the Chattooga River is a spectacular destination.

<u>What to look for:</u> The river begins about 10 miles north of the state border and joins forces with the East Fork 2 miles into the state, near the Walhalla Fish Hatchery. Within the next 40 miles, the river falls more than 2,000 feet, creating some of the best whitewater recreation in the Southeast. Between rapids and waterfalls are smooth stretches inviting contemplation and relaxation ... with or without a fishing rod in hand. The river is treacherous, with landmarks bearing names such as "Decapi-tation Rock" making it advisable to paddle with an experienced guide. Portions of the Bartram and Chattooga trails follow the river and lead into the Ellicott Rock Wilderness Area. For trail information, consult the USDA Forest Service. Several

Within 40 miles the Chattooga River falls more than 2,000 feet, offering excellent whitewater recreation. Photo by Phillip Jones.

parking areas near the river make it possible to visit without a long hike: consider stopping at Burrells Ford, off SC 107, at the SC 28 crossing, or at the Chattooga River Information Station located at the US 76 bridge. Here, the 0.4-mile Bull Sluice Trail provides views of some of the most exciting whitewater on the river. The best trout fishing is generally found above the SC 28 bridge, where the river is closed to boaters. Ospreys fish here, too. Look (or listen) for other raptors like red-tailed and red-shouldered hawks, American kestrels, and barred, screech and great-horned owls. Songbirds are plentiful in the river corridor, with Swainson's and black-throated green warblers, scarlet tanagers, ovenbirds, and indigo buntings keeping birders alert. Wildflower enthusiasts will want to look for swamp *Boykinia*, gay-wing milkwort, yellow lady's slipper, nodding trillium, galax and many others.

<u>When to go:</u> High water in the spring will make paddling more exciting, while lower fall water levels may allow for a slower passage to admire leaf color. Some roads in the area may be impassable during inclement weather.

<u>How to get there:</u> From Clemson, take US 76 toward Westminster and on to the river. There is a parking area on the right before the crossing. You can also take US 76 to Seneca, then turn north on SC 28 toward Walhalla. Both parking and boat access are available on the SC side of the river.

<u>Extras:</u> For information on outfitters or trail maps, call the USDA Forest Service at (864) 638-9568.

2 Buzzards Roost Heritage Preserve

The 1-mile loop trail to the top of Buzzards Roost Mountain offers spectacular scenery, pretty wildflowers, interesting native plants and a private hiking experience not too far from "civilization." The trail is moderate to strenuous, but you don't have to walk the entire length to appreciate the beauty of the area.

<u>What to look for:</u> Black and turkey vultures gave the area its name, but the Heritage Trust Program sought the property because it has the best marble outcrop in the state, creating soil conditions that support a number of rare plants. Among them are ferns — purple cliff-brake, little ebony spleenwort, and woolly lip-fern and smooth coneflower, bindweed, and stoneroot. Less rare, but just as lovely, are mountain laurel, daisies, verbena, yarrow and other wildflowers at the site. As you hike the trail, watch for evidence of black bears, bobcats and other mammals. Wild turkeys and songbirds like rose-breasted grosbeaks, hooded and pine warblers, and ovenbirds breed here. It's also a good place to look for reptiles: lizards, box turtles and an occasional timber rattlesnake. Hikers should remember that in the fall, these snakes tend to congregate and spend the winter in deep rock crevices.

<u>When to go:</u> Fall color peaks in October. The preserve is open during daylight hours. The woods get dark before the mountaintop does, so give yourself plenty of time to negotiate the steep trail back to the road.

<u>How to get there:</u> From Walhalla, go north on SC 28 for 6 miles and turn left on Whetstone Road. Drive approximately 0.75 mile and turn left on Cassidy Bridge Road. After 1 mile, turn left on Rich Mountain Road (Forest Service Road F744) and go about 3 miles to road F744I. Follow this road for 1.1 miles to a one-car pull-off at the trail head. Be careful on the narrow dirt and gravel roads.

<u>Extras:</u> For information about the preserve or the state's Heritage Trust Program, call (803) 734-3893.

Lush vegetation in this mountain setting provides for a myriad of wildlife species, making this preserve a nature viewing haven.
Photo by Robert Clark.

3 Sumter National Forest - Andrew Pickens District

The Andrew Pickens District encompasses much of South Carolina's truly mountainous land, and includes waterfalls, springs, wilderness areas, exciting whitewater opportunities, miles of trails, and 15 recreational areas, four of which allow camping.

<u>What to look for:</u> Because the district covers about 83,000 acres, nearly any plant or animal found in the mountains can be found here. There are many good trout streams, some supporting naturally reproducing populations. Black bears, deer, wild turkeys, beavers and river otters all live here, as do many songbirds and birds of prey. One bird you may hear but probably won't see is the ruffed grouse. Stop by the Stumphouse Ranger Station for maps, brochures and advice. The nearby Yellow Branch Picnic Area includes a 0.1-mile loop trail to Yellow Branch Creek. Picnic areas at Burrells Ford and Moody Springs offer access to waterfalls and springs. The Chattooga Recreation Area, next to the Walhalla Fish Hatchery, offers access to Ellicott Rock Wilderness Area, the East Fork of the Chattooga and the hatchery itself. Cherry Hill Recreation Area, north of Oconee State Park on SC 107, is wheelchair accessible, and has 29 campsites, restrooms, showers and a dump station. Whetstone Horse Camp is designed to serve the needs of riders on the 28-mile Rocky Gap/Willis Knob Horse Trail, which crosses the Chattooga River into Georgia. Nothing but foot traffic is permitted in the 7,012-acre Ellicott Rock Wilderness. Trails lead to Ellicott Rock — believed to be surveyor Andrew Ellicott's marker at the point where Georgia, North Carolina and South Carolina meet. Primitive camping is allowed, with restrictions, and a map is recommended. The Chattooga River Information Station located at the US 76 bridge provides views of some of the most exciting whitewater on the river via the 0.4-mile Bull Sluice trail.

Sumter National Forest safeguards vast expanses of forested mountain lands filled with breathtaking scenery.
Photo by Robert Clark.

<u>When to go:</u> The Stumphouse Ranger Station is open Monday through Friday from 8 a.m. to 4:30 p.m. The office may also be open on Saturdays from early May until the end of August.

<u>How to get there:</u> The Ranger Station is about 6 miles north of Walhalla on SC 28. Consult a map for other destinations, many of which are on or near SC 107.

<u>Extras:</u> For maps or information, call the Andrew Pickens District at (864) 638-9568, or the USDA Forest Service office in Columbia at (803) 561-4000.

4   Oconee State Park

Oconee State Park is a perfect base from which to explore the Chattooga River and other nature-viewing attractions in the northwest corner of the state. It's also a good destination all by itself, with camping, trails, lakes and lush forests.

What to look for: Yet another piece of over-farmed land brought back to life by the Civilian Conservation Corps (CCC), Oconee's thick forests now shelter wildlife and wildflowers in abundance. Look for birds like pileated woodpeckers, Louisiana waterthrushes, black-and-white and worm-eating warblers and scarlet tanagers. Wood ducks nest in boxes on the park's lakes, while migrating ring-necked ducks and spotted sandpipers

An easy trail winds around Oconee State Park, one of many state parks built by the Civilian Conservation Corps during the Depression years. Photo by Ted Borg.

occasionally stop in spring and winter. When hiking the trails, watch for evidence of deer, black bears, and bobcats, and listen for the drumming of ruffed grouse, fairly common but infrequently seen residents. Wildflower enthusiasts will want to watch for dwarf crested irises, galax, soapwort gentians and cranefly orchids. Sourwoods, red maples and scarlet oaks give the woods an especially bright color in the fall. Several trails begin near the cabin area, including the well-known Foothills Trail. A moderate two- to three-hour hike will take you to Hidden Falls, a 60-foot waterfall. Allow two to three hours to hike the Oconee Trail, an easy walk past the lake with optional side trips to a nature-viewing area and the old waterwheel built to serve the CCC camp. If you prefer water to woods, try the easy 0.6-mile walk around the lake. Maps of all trails are available at the park.

When to go: The park is open from 7 a.m. until 7 p.m. November through March and until 9 p.m. April through October. Migrating songbirds and wildflowers will be most prevalent from April through mid-May, while fall color usually peaks in October.

How to get there: From Walhalla, drive north on SC 28, then bear right on SC 107.

Extras: Fish year-round, swim and rent paddle boats or canoes in season. "Trading post," 140 campsites and 19 cabins. For information call (864) 638-5353.

Here's a chance to see "the one that got away" — before it's even released into a stream or river! Kids love to watch the fish dart up and down the long raceways, while parents are equally intrigued by the process that helps keep trout swimming in cool Upstate waters. The Sumter National Forest Chattooga Picnic Area is adjacent to the hatchery.

What to look for: The DNR releases fish raised at the Walhalla Hatchery into cold-water streams and rivers in South Carolina, where heavy fishing pressure and low nutrient levels combine to limit natural trout populations. Most hatchery visitors take advantage of the trails, benches and shade provided by ancient trees in the Chattooga Picnic Area to eat a sandwich, contemplate the river, or take a 30-minute loop trail into the serenity of Ellicott Rock Wilderness Area. Those interested in a longer hike can take a 2.5-mile trail to the main channel of the Chattooga River, then hike 1.7 miles upstream to Ellicott Rock where South Carolina, North Carolina and Georgia meet. The picnic area offers a wheelchair-accessible fishing pier over the East Fork of the Chattooga River.

When to go: The hatchery is open between 8 a.m. and 4 p.m. daily, with the exception of Christmas Day, when the facility opens at noon. Inclement winter weather may cause unexpected closures. The best time to schedule a tour is fall, when more stages in the life cycle of the trout, including eggs and sac fry, can be seen.

How to get there: Take SC 28 north from Walhalla, then turn on SC 107, following signs to Oconee State Park. The hatchery is about 8 miles north of the park, on the left. The road leading from SC 107 to the hatchery and picnic area is paved but quite steep.

Extras: Good interpretive material and brochure. Wheelchair-accessible restrooms available during regular hatchery hours. For group tours, call DNR at (864) 638-2866. For information about the fishing pier or picnic area, call the U.S. Forest Service at (864) 638-9568.

The DNR stocks more than 300,000 trout into South Carolina waters each year.
Photo by Ted Borg.

6   Foothills Trail

The Foothills Trail and its spurs link Oconee, Table Rock, Caesars Head and Jones Gap state parks, making 120 miles of spectacular scenery and abundant wildlife accessible to serious hikers. Because it is close to major metropolitan areas and intersects several roads, most of the trail is also accessible to day-hikers, anglers and casual visitors. Many of the best nature-viewing sites in the mountains are on, or close to, the Foothills Trail.

<u>What to look for:</u> Scenery along the trail is spectacular, with views of mountains and valleys, Lake Jocassee, river rapids and waterfalls. Upper and Lower Whitewater Falls together form one of the longest waterfalls east of the Rockies, but the trail passes many other equally beautiful falls. Because the trail crosses such varied terrain, hikers can see many different forest types, ranging from Appalachian coves with groves of giant hemlocks, some five feet in diameter, to dry ridges dominated by chestnut oaks and pitch pine. Wildflowers bloom in abundance, especially in the spring. As would be expected in an area with minimal human disturbance, a rich array of birds, mammals, reptiles and amphibians flourishes. A healthy population of black bears lives in the vicinity of the trail. Deer and wild turkeys are also common but, like the bears, not likely to be seen unless you're an early riser. You may hear the drumming of ruffed grouse during the spring and early summer. Hawk migrations, viewed from the trail on Sassafras Mountain (the highest point in SC), are a sight not soon forgotten. Other birds of prey to watch for include eagles near Lake Jocassee and peregrine falcons at Table Rock State Park. Rainbow and brown trout reproduce naturally in most of the major streams crossed by the trail.

Enchanting waterfalls along the Foothills Trail make ideal resting spots for hikers.
Photo by Robert Clark.

South Carolina Heritage Corridor

Stretching from Oconee County in the northwest corner of the state to Charleston, the Heritage Corridor highlights the state's cultural and natural history and offers a glimpse of vanishing lifestyles. The "Discovery Route" links many of the corridor's significant historic sites and settlements, while the "Nature Route" offers travelers access to a wide range of outdoor experiences. Regional Discovery Centers and Regional Trails will provide information about local bed-and-breakfasts, restaurants, attractions and resources. Many of the sites included in this guide are within the corridor. For more information about the corridor and affiliated accommodations, please call (803) 734-0344.

Above: *Pink lady slippers* (Cypripedium acaule) *are among several orchid species found in South Carolina. Photo by Michael Foster.* Below: *Black bears* (Ursus americanus) *are seldom seen; attentive hikers are more apt to find tracks or other signs of their presence. Photo by Phillip Jones.*

When to go: Wildflowers will be most plentiful in spring, leaf color best in fall. Winter weather may make some trails difficult to negotiate.

How to get there: Access the trail at points along its route. Serious hikers should contact the Foothills Trail Conference for a guide. Day-hikers can get a feel for the trail by entering at either the Oconee or Table Rock trail heads, by parking at Sassafras Mountain, Chimneytop Gap (both off Secondary Road 199 in Pickens County), or the Eastatoe Gorge spur trail (off US 178 in Pickens County), or by parking at the Bad Creek Whitewater Falls/Foothills Trail Access Area off SC 130 in Oconee County.

Extras: For information call the Foothills Trail Conference at (864) 467-9537.

7   Bad Creek/Lower Whitewater River

Most hikes don't start at a hydroelectric facility — but then, most hydro facilities don't have hiking trails. This one does! A scenic overlook allows for quiet contemplation of a panorama that stretches from Lower Whitewater Falls to the southern end of Lake Jocassee, while the Whitewater River/Foothills Trail Access Area serves as the gateway to some of the best hiking trails in the region.

What to look for: After registering at the gate, head toward the visitors' overlook to get your bearings. As you face Lake Jocassee, Lower Whitewater Falls will be on your left. Then, leave your car at the Whitewater River/Foothills Trail Access Area parking lot and take a 0.6-mile walk through beautiful woods to join the Foothills Trail or one of two spur trails. (One spur leads up Coon Branch, while the other leads to a spot overlooking Lower Whitewater Falls.) The Whitewater River and its tributary Coon Branch shelter rare species and unusual biological communities, huge trees and a wealth of wildlife. As you hike toward the river, look for interesting plants like running

Stretching from neighboring North Carolina, the Whitewater River flows into scenic Lake Jocassee. Photo by Phillip Jones.

cedar and wildflowers ranging from tiny wild ginger to tall deciduous azaleas. Migrant songbirds fill the woods in spring and fall while many resident birds make a home here year-round. Eagles, ospreys, and other birds of prey are often seen soaring over Lake Jocassee or nearby forests. The cool woods surrounding Coon Branch are a special haven for salamanders and other amphibians, although the Whitewater and Thompson rivers have their share as well. This is a good spot to look for bobcats and black bears — both are plentiful in the area.

When to go: The facility is always open, but you should plan to hike during daylight hours. Wildflowers will be more plentiful in the spring, while fall color will peak in October.

How to get there: The Bad Creek project is approximately 10 miles north of the intersection of SC 11 and SC 130, on SC 130. Turn right and register with the guard before entering.

Extras: Portable toilets and telephone located in Whitewater River/Foothills Trail Access Area parking lot. Visitor Center open June to August, 10 a.m. to 5 p.m. Thursday through Saturday, and noon to 5 p.m. Sunday. For more information call (864) 885-4600.

Devils Fork attracts an interesting mix of anglers and wildflower-seekers, boaters and campers, all of whom leave with an appreciation for the beauty of Lake Jocassee.

<u>What to look for:</u> Lake Jocassee is known for its game fish, especially record-breaking trout. It's also known as one of the few public properties where the Oconee bells occur naturally. When these plants of federal concern are in bloom, generally in mid-March, people come from around the country to see and photograph them. The mile-long Oconee Bell Nature Trail is a good place to look for other wildflowers too, like rosebay rhododendron, mountain laurel, cranefly orchid, whorled loosestrife, dwarf crested iris, flame azalea and horse sugar. The trail begins behind the parking area at the park store/ranger station and winds its way through woods filled with songbirds. Look for scarlet tanagers, wood thrushes, red-eyed vireos, ovenbirds and warblers. The open shoreline offers great views of this mountain lake. When it's quiet, you may enjoy common loons, horned grebes, Canada geese and wood ducks, as well as great blue and green herons. In winter, look for bald eagles, Bonaparte's and ring-billed gulls. You may also see peregrine falcons, ospreys and broad-winged hawks. Look for signs of black bears and deer throughout the area.

<u>When to go:</u> On weekdays, the park is open from 7 a.m. to 9 p.m. during daylight-saving time, and until 7 p.m. during the remainder of the year. The park is open from 7 a.m. until 9 p.m. on Friday and Saturday year-round. Oconee bells typically bloom in mid-March, bird life is at its best in spring and fall, and winter is the best time to see bald eagles, common loons and horned grebes.

<u>How to get there:</u> Devils Fork is 5 miles north of Salem, off SC 11, on Jocassee Lake Road and 15 miles northwest of Pickens. Signs on SC 11 will direct you to the park via S-25 or S-127.

<u>Extras:</u> Four boat landings, 20 villas, 59 RV sites and 20 walk-in tent camping sites. Lake fishing available all year; lake swimming an option during the warmer months. Wildflower exhibit in park store. For information call (864) 944-2639.

Rare Oconee bells (Shortia galacifolia) *can be seen growing in their preferred habitat along Devils Fork Park trails.* Photos by Michael Foster.

23

9 Keowee-Toxaway State Park

Although sometimes overshadowed by its older and better-known neighbors, Keowee-Toxaway should be included on any visit to the mountain parks. The museum and interpretive trail tell the story of the Cherokee from their arrival in the Blue Ridge to the present, while challenging trails and abundant wildlife make the trip worth the time of any hiker or amateur naturalist.

<u>What to look for:</u> The history of South Carolina is almost inseparable from that of the Cherokee Nation, a fact made clear by the excellent exhibits at the park. Begin at the museum, then walk the 0.25-mile interpretive trail, which tells the story of the Cherokee in four separate exhibits. For more serious hiking, cross SC 11 to the north section of the park and take the Raven Rock Hiking Trail or the Natural Bridge Nature Trail. The 4.2-mile round trip to Raven Rock is rated moderate to strenuous, while the Natural Bridge Nature Trail is more moderate and can be walked in about an hour. Along the way, you'll pass creeks and waterfalls and may see raptors like bald eagles, ospreys, and, in summer, broad-winged and sharp-shinned hawks. A peregrine falcon makes an occasional appearance. Native plant enthusiasts will want to watch for the Allegheny-spurge, a plant of regional concern, and wildflowers such as Catesby's trillium, rosebud orchid and rosebay rhododendron.

<u>When to go:</u> The park is open daily from 9 a.m. until 9 p.m. April through October. During the remainder of the year, it closes at 8 p.m. on Friday and at 6 p.m. Saturday through Thursday. The museum is open during park office hours: 11 a.m. to noon and 4 p.m. to 5 p.m. Fall color generally peaks in late October, while wildflowers are most abundant in spring, especially along the Natural Bridge Nature Trail.

A bald eagle (Haliaeetus leucocephalus) *soars above Lake Keowee.* Photo by Phillip Jones.

<u>How to get there:</u> Keowee-Toxaway spans SC 11 on the east side of Lake Keowee. The park is just west of the intersection of SC 11 and SC 133. The entrance to the museum, picnic areas and interpretive trail is on the south side of the highway, while the longer hiking trails begin on the north side.

<u>Extras:</u> Small number of campsites and one cabin available. Museum gift shop has good selection of books about the Cherokees, with many intended for children or young people. For information call (864) 868-2605.

Laurel Fork Heritage Preserve is part of Jocassee Gorges, a 39,500-acre natural area acquired by the state and The Conservation Fund from Duke Energy's Crescent Resources. Laural Fork Heritage Preserve was the first tract of land purchased by the state in the Jocassee Gorges project.

What to look for: The flora and fauna of the Southern Appalachians are among the most diverse in North America. This is especially true within the Blue Ridge Escarpment, where elevations plunge 2,000 feet within a short distance and rainfall is very high. Laurel Fork Heritage Preserve is located just west of the Eastatoe Creek Heritage Preserve and contains trout streams, river gorges and a waterfall. Rare animal species located on the property include the wood rat, Appalachian cottontail and red squirrel. Rare plant species include pipevine, Oconee bells, yellow violet and evergreen woodfern. Among the many reptiles and amphibians residing here are several that are rare for this area, including green salamanders and wood and pickerel frogs. The Foothills Trail, an 80-mile footpath running between Oconee State Park and Table Rock State park, traverses Laurel Fork Heritage Preserve, making possible dayhikes or backpacking excursions of several days in length.

The Jocassee watershed includes the state's highest concentration of rare and endangered species. Photo by Phillip Jones.

When to go: The scenery will be beautiful any time of year. More wildflowers will be blooming in spring, while fall foliage normally peaks around the third week in October.

How to get there: From SC 11, head north on US 178 toward Rocky Bottom. Keep heading north after passing Rocky Bottom. Just after crossing Eastatoe Bridge, turn left on Horsepasture Road. Look for the Foothills Trail parking area on this road.

Extras: For information about Laurel Fork Heritage Preserve or about the state's Heritage Trust Program, call (803) 734-3893. For a Foothills Trail map, call the Foothills Trail Conference at (864) 467-9537. For information about hunting and fishing opportunities within Jocassee Gorges, call (864) 654-1671.

11 Eastatoe Creek Heritage Preserve

It's hard to reach, but worth the effort. Three creeks flow into the Eastatoe, which then drops 600 feet before roaring through the narrow rock walls of Eastatoe Gorge. The resulting spray creates humid conditions that enable three species of rare ferns to thrive. One of these is found nowhere else in North America.

A 2.5-mile walk to the bottom of Eastatoe Gorge rewards the hiker with spectacular scenery.
Photo by Robert Clark.

What to look for: The main attraction here is water pouring through the gorge, in one place only three feet wide. However, the 2.5-mile hike to the bottom of the gorge provides opportunities to cross a variety of habitats, with associated wildlife and plants. The trail begins along an old logging road, where the open habitat favors species like deer, cottontail rabbits, indigo buntings and prairie warblers. As the trail descends, it enters deeper forests where ruffed grouse might be heard. Look for black-and-white warblers. Near the bottom of the gorge, the trail passes through stands of rhododendron and hemlock, some of which are quite large. At the base of the trail the high moisture levels produce spectacular wildflower shows. Sixteen species of violet live here, as do foamflowers, saxifrages, Carolina geraniums, wake robins and other trilliums. Copperheads, the most common venomous snake in the state, seem to be exceptionally common here. Remember that snakes, like all other wildlife, are protected in the preserve.

When to go: The preserve is open during daylight hours. Wildflowers will be most prevalent in the spring, while fall is the best time for leaf color, but the preserve is fascinating any time of year.

How to get there: From the intersection of SC 11 and US 178 in Holly Springs, go north on US 178 about 8 miles, passing through Rocky Bottom. After crossing the bridge over Eastatoe Creek, turn left onto the dirt road (not the paved road). Drive 0.2 mile to the Foothills Trail parking area on the left and walk up the road about 1/8 mile to the trail head.

Extras: Trail is narrow, steep and strenuous in parts. Be prepared for wet feet. Primitive campsites at end of trail. For information about the preserve or the state's Heritage Trust Program, call (803) 734-3893.

One of South Carolina's most widely recognized natural features is Table Rock Mountain, named by Cherokees who imagined the Great Spirit sitting on nearby Stool Mountain and dining at the "Table." However, unless you've visited the park, you've missed its softer side — lakes and waterfalls, trails and forests.

What to look for: The scenery is some of the best in the Upstate. Picturesque and accessible waterfalls captivate children and adults alike, while strenuous trails leading to Table Rock or to Pinnacle Mountain offer spectacular views. The predominantly hardwood forest attracts many songbirds and provides habitat for black bears, bobcats and other mammals, as well as a host of reptiles, amphibians and insects. Wildflowers fill the woods, as do flowering shrubs such as flame azaleas and mountain laurel. All trails begin at the Nature Center near Pinnacle Lake and pass by a series of waterfalls. Then you must choose between the 1.9-mile Carrick Creek Nature Trail loop, the 3.4-mile Table Rock trail (two to three hours one way) or the 3.3-mile hike to the top of Pinnacle Mountain (two to three hours one way). The Foothills Trail begins here and ends 80 miles and several days later at Oconee State Park.

When to go: The park is open from 7 a.m. to 9 p.m. Spring and fall are the best times to see migrating birds. Spring is also the best time to see wildflowers, while fall color is likely to peak in late October.

How to get there: The park is 12 miles north of Pickens on SC 11. The east gate leads to the Lodge Restaurant, while the west gate provides access to nature center, trails and other facilities. To boat (electric-motor only) on 67-acre Lake Oolenoy, enter across SC 11 from the west gate road.

Extras: Pedal boats and swimming (in season), fishing, 75 campsites, 14 cabins available for rent. Nature programs. Hikers must register at nature center. Entrance fee. Call (864) 878-9813 for information.

Table Rock, seen here from Caesars Head, was a sacred place to Native Americans. South Carolinians are still awed by its majesty. Photo by Phillip Jones.

13 Mountain Bridge Wilderness and Recreation Area

The Mountain Bridge joins the watersheds of Table Rock Reservoir and Poinsett Reservoir with a "bridge" of undeveloped land. Currently, its 12,000 acres encompass Caesars Head and Jones Gap state parks, and three Heritage Preserves: Watson, Eva Russell Chandler and Ashmore.

<u>What to look for:</u> No one should pass near Caesars Head State Park without stopping to marvel at the view of Table Rock and the Blue Ridge beyond. On a clear day, you can sometimes see mountains in Georgia. At Jones Gap, the Middle Saluda River and Cleveland Cliff provide the spectacular scenery. Hiking trails lead along the Middle Saluda River, past waterfalls and lush Appalachian cove forests. The Middle Saluda was the state's first designated Scenic River, and it lives up to its name, whether you hike beside it, listen to its rushing waters as you picnic in the park, or merely glimpse it from the road. Jones Gap Trail is one of the easier trails in the Mountain Bridge, and those who hike it will be rewarded with views of the river, huge trees, wildflowers and abundant wildlife. A number of trails also cross the area. Raven Cliff Falls, the best-known of the waterfalls in the vicinity, drops 420 feet, making it one of the tallest in the eastern U.S. Look for the beginning of the 4.6-mile (round trip) trail 1 mile north of the Caesars Head State Park headquarters. The three Heritage Preserves encompassed by the Mountain Bridge protect rare plant species and unusual communities, including cataract bogs and a montane bog. Cataract bogs form where a permanent stream flows over a steeply sloped rock outcrop. They can be very slick and dangerous. Hikers should stand back to protect both themselves and the fragile plant community. Among the rare or significant plant species sheltered in the three preserves are Indian paint brush, grass-of-Parnassus, painted trillium and swamp pink. Watson Heritage Preserve contains two mountain streams with wild populations of brook trout, the state's only native trout species. Ashmore is home to three wildlife species of special concern: the green salamander, Rafinesque's big-eared bat and the wood rat.

Left: *The roaring waters of Raven Cliff Falls plummet 420 feet, a natural wonder and thrilling spectacle.* Above: *Rim of the Gap Trail offers a challenge to the adventurous hiker.* Right: *Wake robin* (Trillium erectum) *is one member of the lily family decorating the Mountain Bridge in spring.* Photos by Phillip Jones.

When to go: The Mountain Bridge Wilderness headquarters and information center at the Caesars Head State Park store is open from 9 a.m. to 6 p.m. daily, as is the park itself during fall and winter. From April to September the park (but not the store) stays open until 9 p.m. Heritage Preserves are open during daylight hours.

How to get there: Caesars Head State Park is on US 276 northwest of Greenville, near the North Carolina/South Carolina border. To reach Jones Gap State Park, take SC 11 north from Cleveland and turn right (north) on S-23-97, which parallels the Middle Saluda River. Both the Ashmore and Chandler heritage preserves are on Persimmon Ridge Road, 3.9 miles west of the junction of SC 11 and US 276. The Watson preserve can be reached by hiking the Gum Gap Trail section of the Foothills Trail, beginning at the Raven Cliff Falls parking area. To drive to the preserve, take US 276 about 5 miles north of the North Carolina/South Carolina state line, into North Carolina, and turn left on East Fork Road. Drive 1.4 miles and turn left on Happy Acres (a dirt and gravel road). Follow Happy Acres for 1.7 miles, where it forks. The road to the preserve is on the right and leads to a gate and parking pull-off within 0.2 miles.

Extras: Primitive camping is allowed in Jones Gap State Park and on Watson Heritage Preserve. For information about the Mountain Bridge Wilderness and Recreation Area, call (864) 836-6115. For information about the Heritage Preserves or the state's Heritage Trust Program, call (803) 734-3893. "Mountain Bridge Trails," published by Naturaland Trust, is available at Caesars Head State Park and at many book stores.

14 Glassy Mountain Heritage Preserve

Although the preserve protects a rare plant community, it is the breathtaking view from the top of this Piedmont monadnock that brings people to Glassy Mountain. From the trail on the north side of the mountain, you can look out over Table Rock, Caesars Head and points beyond, or down nearly 400 feet of steep rock face to the farmland below.

What to look for: The monadnock, or isolated mountain, is an extraordinary sight, rising as it does from the relatively flat surrounding landscape. You can get a good look at the steep north face of the mountain from SC 8, north of Pickens. Then, hike the 0.6-mile moderate to strenuous trail, which winds around the east side of the mountain before reaching the bare dome and extraordinary views on the north side. From the dome, a

Serene, scenic views are an added treat for those who scale this remarkable monadnock. Photo by Ted Borg.

short, steep climb through beautiful chestnut oaks and other hardwoods brings you to a SC Forestry Commission fire tower at the end of South Glassy Mountain Road. Return to the trail head via the road. A delicate plant community softens the bare granite of the dome. Among the plants growing here is the regionally threatened thousandleaf groundsel. Wildflowers to watch for along the trail include various spiderworts, Indian pinks, bluets, Solomon's seal and bluestar. From the trail, you may see birds of prey soaring over the farmland and may hear an occasional bobwhite quail. If you hear scurrying in leaves, it's probably one of several species of lizard or a chipmunk.

When to go: The preserve is open during daylight hours. Be careful during wet weather, as the trail may be slick.

How to get there: From SC 8 in Pickens, take SC 183 east about 1.5 miles. Turn left (north) on South Glassy Mountain Road and continue to the intersection with Glassy Mountain Church Road. The trail begins on the right, about 200 feet farther along South Glassy Mountain Road. It rejoins the paved road at the top of the mountain.

Extras: For information about the preserve or the state's Heritage Trust Program, call (803) 734-3893.

To protect one of the few remaining undisturbed habitats for the federally endangered bunched arrowhead, the DNR acquired property upstream from the seeps where the plant grows — a gain for the plant and the public! Easy trails leading through the property offer a pretty hike and an opportunity to see various wildlife management techniques at work.

What to look for: The 1.25-mile trail skirts a wild plum thicket in an open field, then parallels a stream through mixed pine and hardwood forest. Here, where two habitats come together, expect to see a variety of birds. Standouts on the preserve include indigo buntings, acadian flycatchers, yellow-throated vireos and yellow-breasted chats, as well as more commonly seen birds like Carolina wrens and purple martins. Wildflowers ranging from tiny white violets to dwarf heartleaf, Solomon's seal and false Solomon's seal grow along the trail, while running cedar carpets the ground under the trees. As the trail leaves the woods to skirt the open fields, watch for butterflies like silver spotted skippers and red admirals, and upland birds like bobwhite quail and mourning doves. Kestrels and red-tailed and red-shouldered hawks may leave the trees to search for prey in the open areas. Nest boxes dot the entire preserve — look for huge squirrel boxes, as well as owl, bat and the more typical bluebird boxes that attract a variety of cavity nesters.

When to go: The preserve gates are open from 7:30 a.m. until 7:30 p.m. April 1 through August 31. During the rest of the year, the gates are opened at 8 a.m. and locked at 6 p.m.

How to get there: Take US 25/276 north from Greenville. When the two routes diverge, take US 25. Turn right on Tigerville Road. Turn left on Shelton Road. After crossing a small bridge, turn right on McCauley Road. The preserve gate will be on the right.

Extras: Come prepared for abundant poison ivy and ticks. For information about the site or the state's Heritage Trust Program, call (803) 734-3893.

The star of the preserve, the federally endangered bunched arrowhead (Sagittaria fasciculata) *in its natural habitat.* Photo by Ted Borg.

16 Paris Mountain State Park

This 2,000-foot mountain has been protected since 1890, allowing stands of large trees and rare plants to thrive. Its natural lake and picnic areas offer Upstate families a relaxing spot, while the strenuous hiking and mountain-bike trails attract more rugged nature lovers.

Lake Placid offers a good place to look for several different bird species. Photo by Ted Borg.

What to look for: Several state champion trees hide among the old-growth shortleaf, Virginia and table mountain pines, white oaks, northern red oaks and striped maples. Sourwood and mountain laurel bloom profusely during the late spring. Rare plants found here include white goldenrod and Carolina tassel-rue. Many songbirds pass through the park during spring and fall migrations, while others, such as pine, yellow-throated and hooded warblers, ovenbirds, red-eyed vireos and wood thrushes, breed here. Canada geese often choose to nest near busy Lake Placid, where children can admire the goslings from a safe distance. Killdeer and great blue and green herons are year-round residents, and spotted and solitary sandpipers pass through during their annual migrations.

When to go: The park is open from 9 a.m. until 9 p.m. April to September. During the remainder of the year, the park closes at 6 p.m. Saturday through Thursday, and at 8 p.m. on Friday. Wildflowers will be at their best in the spring, mountain laurel peaks in May, and fall color should be best in October.

How to get there: Drive 6 miles north of Greenville on SC 253. From I-385, take SC 291 north to SC 253. Turn right on SC 253 and go 4 miles to State Park Road. The park is on the left.

Extras: Mile-long nature trail (interpretive brochure available) circles Lake Placid, beginning at main picnic area. Hiking trails begin at Sulphur Springs Picnic Area. Brissey Ridge Trail (2.3 miles) and Sulphur Springs Trail (4 miles) rated strenuous. Fire Tower Road is a 1.5-mile mountain-bike trail. Pedal boats and lake swimming available in season. 50 campsites and a group camp. Park is located on land settled by first European sent to trade with Cherokees. Seasonal entrance fee. For information, call (864) 244-5565.

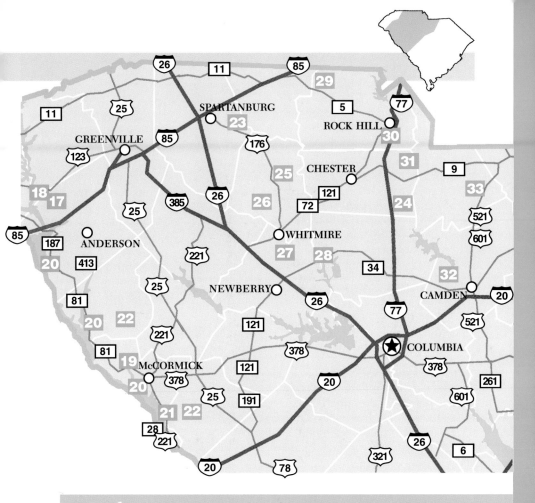

Piedmont

17 SC Botanical Gardens
18 Clemson/Fant's Grove
19 John de la Howe
20 Savannah District Lakes
21 Stevens Creek
    Heritage Preserve
22 Sumter National Forest -
    Long Cane District
23 Pacolet River
    Heritage Preserve
24, 25 Turkey Management -
    Chester, Union Counties
26 Rose Hill Plantation
    State Park
27 Sumter National Forest -
    Enoree Ranger District
28 Lake Monticello/
    Parr Reservoir/
    Broad River

29 Kings Mountain
    State Park
30 Rock Hill Blackjacks
    Heritage Preserve
31 Landsford Canal
    State Park
32 Lake Wateree Dam
33 Flat Creek
    Heritage Preserve/
    Forty-Acre Rock

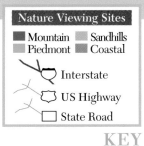

Nature Viewing Sites

- Mountain
- Sandhills
- Piedmont
- Coastal

Interstate
US Highway
State Road

KEY

33

18 Clemson/Fant's Grove Wildlife Management Demonstration Area

Eleven demonstration areas scattered over 8,000 acres provide ample opportunities to see a variety of habitats and to pick up some excellent land management tips. Clemson University and the DNR have developed innovative demonstrations, including a "rabbitat," and a system that allows fields to be used for crops one season, waterfowl habitat the next.

What to look for: Many areas are managed to attract game species like deer, turkey, dove and quail. These same management techniques attract a variety of non-game species, too. River otters and muskrats congregate along the larger creeks and near the beaver pond. Late in the day, watch for deer emerging from the forest.

When to go: Hunting activity is heavier in November, December and April. Site managers recommend visiting before or after hunting season; otherwise, be alert and wear brightly colored clothing. Sites 9 and 11, the waterfowl demonstration areas, are most interesting for bird-watchers from mid-November until March, when up to 23 different waterfowl species are present. The waterfowl demonstration area is only open to the public on Tuesdays and Sundays from a designated observation area; however, all other demonstration areas are open year-round.

How to get there: The Fant's Grove demonstration area begins approximately 3.5 miles south of the Clemson University campus. For a self-guided tour, travel south from campus on US 76. Across from Tri-County Technical College, turn right on S-279 and drive approximately 2 miles. Turn left at Watershed Road, a dirt road closed with a cable. Walk about .25 mile to reach the first site. Other sites can be easily accessed from paved roads; a few require moderate walks.

Side Trip:

#17 South Carolina Botanical Gardens

As you're heading toward the mountains, think about stopping at the South Carolina Botanical Gardens on the Clemson University campus. The woodland walk parallels a small stream and show-cases many mountain and piedmont wildflowers, as well as a few exotic species remaining from the gardens' earlier days. Other trails lead to wetland gardens and to a recreated farmstead. Demonstration gardens will give homeowners ideas, while the newly constructed interpretive center houses a library of materials for the serious gardener. Several outdoor "environmental sculptures" add even more interest. As you approach the Clemson University campus on US 76, watch for signs to the Botanical Gardens on the left. For information call (864) 656-3405.

Extras: Brochure is available. Advanced notice required for group tours. Call (864) 656-4847 or (864) 654-1671 for information.

Bobwhite quail (Colinus virginianus) are quiet as danger approaches; at the last possible moment they burst into the air just underfoot. Photo by Ted Borg

The **John de la Howe School has been serving children** for more than 200 years, but the school is also serving the larger community by inviting the public to visit an interpretive trail through some of its scenic forest.

<u>What to look for:</u> The 1.5-mile trail crosses dry upland hardwood forest, mixed pine/hardwood forest, and some floodplain forest. It overlooks both a two-acre beaver pond and part of the headwaters of Lake Thurmond. Rock outcrops encrusted with lichens are common and add to the beauty of the walk. This is a great place to look for turtles, lizards, toads and other reptiles and amphibians. Birders will appreciate the presence of Eastern wood pewees, red-eyed vireos, wood thrushes, and hooded, yellow, and black-and-white warblers. Near the water, look for great blue herons, egrets, wood ducks and Canada geese. Eagles sometimes pass overhead, as do red-tailed hawks. Listen for quail and turkeys, and the occasional startled deer bounding out of your path. Wildflower enthusiasts should plan a spring trip to see faded trilliums in bloom.

Snapping turtles (Chelydra serpentina) *are a common sight. On warm, sunny days they drift in ponds, awaiting their next meal.* Photo by Phillip Jones.

<u>When to go:</u> The trail is always open, but if you visit on Saturday, you can also visit "The Barn" where volunteers sell student-made crafts and community consignment items. Restrooms and drinking water are only available inside The Barn.

<u>How to get there:</u> From McCormick, go north on SC 28 and follow it for approximately 8 miles. Just after the road crosses the Long Cane Bridge, bear left on SC 81. Watch for The Barn about 3 miles farther on the right, shortly after the main entrance (on the left) to the John de la Howe School. The trail begins at the far side of the field, on the right as you face The Barn.

<u>Extras:</u> Call the school at (864) 391-2131 for information.

20 Savannah District Lakes

The setting sun paints a Lake Hartwell marina in golden tones. Hartwell is named for Revolutionary War heroine Nancy Hart. Photo by Michael Foster.

Often called South Carolina's "freshwater coast," the three lakes built and operated by the U.S. Army Corps of Engineers total 153,000 acres of water, surrounded by 128,000 acres of public land.

What to look for: Lakes Hartwell, Russell and Thurmond (formerly Clarks Hill) punctuate the Savannah River from Oconee County in the north to McCormick County in the Midlands. Lands surrounding the lakes are actively managed for wildlife, with more than 150 food plots around Lake Thurmond alone. Cooperative agreements between the Corps, DNR and organizations such as the Sierra Club, National Audubon Society, National Wild Turkey Federation, Ducks Unlimited and Quail Unlimited also help to focus attention on wildlife. Some 130 parks and other recreation areas make it easy to find just the right spot for fishing, boating or loafing. Lake Hartwell and Sadlers Creek state parks on Hartwell Lake, Calhoun Falls State Park on Lake Russell, and Hickory Knob, Baker Creek and Hamilton Branch state parks on Lake Thurmond provide water access, camping and fishing opportunities. The Corps of Engineers at Hartwell Lake offers camping opportunities at Twin Lakes, Coneross, Oconee Point and Springfield. Mt. Carmel, Leroy's Ferry, Hawe's Creek, and Modoc Camp are available at Thurmond Lake. Day-use facilities are also available on Thurmond and Hartwell lakes. Boat landings dot the shores on both sides of the river.

When to go: "The freshwater coast" is always open, but some access points may not be. Check individual lake offices for dates and hours of operation.

How to get there: Let your destination be your guide, but try to incorporate part of the Savannah River Scenic Highway into your trip. It roughly parallels the Savannah River, beginning at the northern end where SC 24 intersects with the Cherokee Foothills Scenic Highway (SC 11), and ending where SC 28 crosses the Savannah River at the Georgia border.

Extras: Maps of each lake and surrounding public lands available. Corps provides outdoor recreational opportunities for disabled sportsmen. Equestrian trails available. Tours of dams and powerhouse facilities may be arranged. For maps, tour information, or information about recreational opportunities, call 1-888-893-0678 for Hartwell, 1-800-944-7207 for Russell, and 1-800-533-3478 for Thurmond.

21   Stevens Creek Heritage Preserve

Noted botanist Dr. Albert Radford, coauthor of *Vascular Flora of the Carolinas*, described this site as "one of the most unique floristic sites in the two Carolinas." Presumed to be a remnant of an ancient glacial period, the area hosts plants from the coastal plain, piedmont and mountains. But even if you don't know a trillium from a trilobite, the site is well worth a visit. Intermittent streams, interesting geology and views of Stevens Creek make the trail a delight in any season.

What to look for: As you follow the trail, you'll cross several forest types. In the winter, you can see for miles from the top of the bluff. At the base of the bluff, fertile soils and cooler temperatures result in an astonishing array of spring wildflowers. Look for false rue anemones, spring beauties, lance-leaved, faded and nodding trilliums, Dutchman's breeches, green violets and may apples. Painted buckeye lines the trail. The Florida gooseberry, a federally endangered species, also grows in this zone. The diverse forest and floodplain habitats attract an assortment of birds, with warblers and woodpeckers being most prominent. Pileated wood-peckers, American redstarts, red-eyed vireos and prothonotary warblers are stand-outs. The rare Webster's salamander lives here, along with many more common amphibians and reptiles.

When to go: The preserve is open from daylight to dusk. Spring wildflowers peak in April and there should be good fall color, too. More birds are present and active early in the morning and late in the afternoon, in spring and fall.

How to get there: From Exit 1 on I-20 in North Augusta, turn north on SC 230. At the intersection with S-19-143, turn left and drive until you cross Stevens Creek. Parking area and trail head are on the right at the top of the hill, just beyond the creek.

Extras: Because of sensitive plant commu-nities in the preserve, hikers must stay on the trail. Trail takes less than an hour to walk; more if you plan to photograph wildflowers. For information on the site or the state's Heritage Trust Program, call (803) 734-3893.

Less than an inch long, the delicate blooms of Dutchman's breeches (Dicentra cucullaria) *are a delightful find in springtime. Photo by Ted Borg.*

22 Sumter National Forest - Long Cane District

Stretching eastward from the shores of Lake Thurmond, the 119,000-acre Long Cane District includes many opportunities to hike, cycle, fish, bird-watch, picnic or swim.

The largest known shagbark hickory (Carya ovata) *in South Carolina is located in a mature forest in the Long Cane Scenic Area. The forest hasn't been cut since 1930.* Photo by Ted Borg.

What to look for: Birds of prey are well represented here. If you visit during breeding season (April to October) you may see prairie warblers or wood thrushes. Look for Bachman's sparrows in loblolly pines during nesting season. Several endangered species are found within the forest, including Webster's salamander and the Carolina heelsplitter mussel. More typical species are here as well; good populations of deer and turkeys roam the forest, and managers hope quail demonstration areas will increase the population of that once-common bird. Unusual plants to watch for include faded trillium, columbo and Oglethorpe oak. The Lick Fork Recreation Area boasts a family camping area, fishing pier, swimming area and bathhouse. Turkey Creek and Stevens Creek offer excellent fishing and floating opportunities enhanced by trails and primitive camping areas. Primitive camping and trails for hikers, equestrians, cyclists and motorcyclists are located in the Parson's Mountain Recreation Area. The 7-mile Long Cane Trail begins here and enters Long Cane Scenic Area.

When to go: The forest is interesting any time of year. Wear brightly colored clothing and be cautious when using the forest during hunting seasons.

How to get there: Several major highways cross the forest. Lick Fork Recreation Area is approximately 11 miles southwest of Edgefield on SC 230, while Parson's Mountain Recreation Area is south of Abbeville off SC 28. Two boat ramps, one with a picnic area, are found on Long Cane Creek off SC 28.

Extras: Call (803) 637-5396 for information about, or maps of, the forest.

Come to bird-watch, photograph, fish or simply enjoy the woods and river. Leave with a sense of awe sparked by visiting a site important to people thousands of years ago. As you sit watching the river, imagine the lives of the Native Americans who stopped here on their seasonal migrations between the coast and the uplands of the state.

<u>What to look for:</u> The preserve protects two Native American soapstone quarries. Early residents of the state came here between 3000 and 1100 B.C. to obtain material from which they made bowls, pipes and other necessities. The soapstone outcrops are fragile and should not be touched. Two uncommon plant species, a moss and a leafy liverwort, are also protected within the preserve. Less rare, but no less interesting, are the pine/hardwoods along the Pacolet River. In summer, the forest shelters wood thrushes, red-eyed vireos, Eastern wood pewees and yellow-billed cuckoos, along with more commonly-seen songbirds. Reptiles and amphibians love the woods, too. Look for harmless black rat snakes and Eastern kingsnakes, as well as gray treefrogs, toads and other amphibians. Allow about 20 minutes to walk the short trail from the parking area to the river.

<u>When to go:</u> The preserve is open from daylight to dusk. Spring and fall are the best times for migrating songbirds, and the hardwoods should produce good fall color.

<u>How to get there:</u> Take US 176/9 east from Spartanburg to S-42-680. Turn left on S-42-680 and follow it to its intersection with S-42-108. Turn right on S-42-108, then left on Bethesda Place Road and follow it to the parking area. Park and walk down the dirt trail.

<u>Extras:</u> For general information about the site or the state's Heritage Trust Program, call (803) 734-3893. For information about the soapstone quarries or other archaeological resources of the state, ask for the Heritage Trust archaeologist at the same number.

White-eyed vireos (Vireo griseus) *will build their elegant, hanging nests in low shrubs and bushes. Lined with lichens and mosses, the nests accomodate as many as five hatchlings per brood.* Photo by Robert Clark.

24, 25 Chester and Union County Wild Turkey Management Demonstration Areas

Want to see wild turkeys without getting up at the crack of dawn? Here is an opportunity to see this elusive native bird in prime habitat, and you'll also see how good land management can make property more attractive to turkeys and other wildlife.

<u>What to look for:</u> Turkeys, of course! You can also see red-tailed hawks, and upland mammals such as raccoons and white-tailed deer. Songbirds typical of the shortleaf/loblolly pine and mixed pine/hardwood forest areas are present as well.

<u>When to go:</u> The sites are open from May 2 until September 30. In general, the best time of day to see turkeys is early morning.

<u>How to get there:</u> The Chester County site is about 4 miles west of Great Falls. From the intersection of I-77 and SC 97, go east (toward Great Falls) and turn left on SC 901. Drive about 4 miles and turn left on Martin Grave Road (dirt). Stop at gates located 0.5 and 0.75 miles down the road on the left. The Union County site is approximately 4 miles east of Union. From Union, take SC 49 north to Monarch Mills. Turn right on the SC 215 Connector and drive approximately 1.5 miles. Turn left on Neal Shoals Road, then left on Fairview Church Road. The demonstration area is approximately 1 mile on both sides of the road. The larger portion is on the right. Foot travel only is the rule at either site. Park at the gate or along the roadside near the gate, walk quietly, and you should see turkeys. Even if you don't see the birds, you'll see ideal turkey habitat and be able to recognize it in other areas. You'll find yourself scanning the fields as you ride through the countryside.

Extras: Demonstration areas are owned by Bowater, Inc. and managed for wild turkeys through a cooperative effort with the DNR and the SC Chapter of the National Wild Turkey Federation. For information on these areas and management techniques, call DNR's regional office in Union at (864) 427-4771.

Not often are visitors treated to such sights, but occasionally white-tailed deer (Odocoileus virginianus) *and Eastern wild turkeys* (Meleagris gallopavo) *do cross paths.*
Photo by Glenn Gardner.

Tucked into the middle of the Sumter National Forest is the home of former Governor William H. Gist, who led the state as it seceded from the Union. Visit the lovely house, outbuildings, and rose gardens that gave the plantation its name, then follow the nature trail to the Tyger River.

What to look for: From the picnic shelter, a 1.5-mile nature trail crosses through an oak/hickory forest, descends to the banks of the Tyger River, then returns to the park. The trail passes a deep gully, a remnant of the damage done by poor farming practices in the past. Although it is beautiful now, with ferns, lichens and other tiny plants thriving in its seeps, one can imagine a day when the land was bare and the gully was nothing but mud. Along the trail, look for snakes, lizards, songbirds and spring

More than sixty rose bushes, including such old-fashioned varieties as "Gaelic" and "Regosa," are found in the park's gardens. One plant is said to trace its origins to a cutting from one of the Gists' original roses. Photo by Michael Foster.

wildflowers. Near the river, you may see wading birds, salamanders, frogs, and very different wildflowers and shrubs than those found in the upland areas of the park. During wet weather, the trail doesn't go all the way to the river — the river meets the trail! If you want to boat this portion of the river, the Sumter National Forest's Rose Hill Boat Landing is just down the road.

When to go: The park is open from 9 a.m. to 6 p.m. Thursday through Monday. The mansion itself is open from 1 p.m. to 4 p.m. on Thursday, Friday and Monday. Tours are offered on Saturday from 10 a.m. until 3 p.m. and on Sunday from noon to 3 p.m. Because the National Forest surrounding the mansion is open for hunting, orange vests or other brightly colored garments are recommended for visits during hunting seasons. During winter or other wet periods, be prepared for parts of the trail to be underwater.

How to get there: The park is about 8 miles south of Union. From US 176, which traverses Sumter National Forest, follow signs to the park, located off Sardis Road.

Extras: Picnic shelters may be reserved. Fee charged to tour mansion. For information, call (864) 427-5966.

27 Sumter National Forest - Enoree Ranger District

These 168,000 acres of woods and rivers provide a green oasis between the population centers of Columbia and Greenville-Spartanburg. The Enoree and Tyger rivers flow in parallel paths across the forest and into the Broad River, creating excellent recreational opportunities.

<u>What to look for</u>: The proximity of dry upland forest to swampy riverbottom forest creates a mix of habitats that attracts a variety of wildlife. Songbirds, birds of prey and game species are found in abundance here. The river bottoms harbor otters, salamanders and frogs. Both the Tyger and Enoree rivers offer great float trip opportunities. Ruins of antebellum houses and historic cemeteries add cultural interest. Molly's Rock Picnic Area, about 10 miles north of Newberry, has a picnic shelter, fishing pier and a 0.6 mile nature trail around a small pond. Woods Ferry Recreation Area in the northeast corner of the district offers 39 campsites, picnic areas, a 10 miles of non-motorized trails for equestrians, hikers and cyclists and a boat ramp providing access to the Broad River. Brickhouse Campground in the southwest part of the district offers 22 campsites, horse corrals, and the trailhead for the 32-mile Buncombe Trail and access to the Sumter passage of the Palmetto Trail. Look for Sedalia, Wildcat, Macedonia and John's Creek lakes off SC 18 in the northwest corner of the District. John's Creek Lake has a fishing pier and Sedalia Lake has a wildlife viewing blind.

<u>When to go:</u> The best wildlife viewing will be in the spring and fall. Woods Ferry Recreation Area is open from Memorial Day until the last Sunday in November. Brickhouse Campground open year-round.

<u>How to get there:</u> Sumter National Forest is easily accessible from I-26 or US 176. Consult a detailed map for directions to specific destinations.

<u>Extras:</u> All fishing piers mentioned are wheel-chair-accessible. For a recreation directory, maps or advice, consult the USDA Forest Service at (803) 276-4810.

White-tailed deer (Odocoileus virginianus) *are abundant in Sumter National Forest. Bucks shed their antlers in winter and regrow them each spring.*
Photo by Phillip Jones.

Lake Monticello and Parr Reservoir are among the state's newest lakes, created to provide cooling water for a nuclear power plant in the late 1970s. The lakes have matured and are now beautiful spots for fishing and bird-watching. The nearby Broad River WMA is a good spot to see heavenly habitat for waterfowl.

What to look for: At the Broad River Waterfowl Management Area wood ducks, mallards, Canada geese, coots and other waterfowl swim lazily, while great blue herons ply the margins of the river. "Great blues" and Canada geese also live on the lakes, as do double-crested cormorants from time to time. Look up and you may see an osprey or even an eagle. The forests along the shorelines are good spots to look for salamanders and various reptiles, especially in the spring.

When to go: Broad River Waterfowl Management Area is open to the public between February 2 and October 31. The best viewing times at Lake Monticello and Parr Reservoir are dawn and dusk during late winter.

How to get there: Lake Monticello can be reached from several spots along US 215. Driving north from Columbia, look for Overlook parking on the left, approximately 4 miles north of Jenkinsville. Or, drive about 3 more miles and follow signs on the left to the public recreation area maintained by S.C. Electric and Gas Co. Here you'll find two boat ramps, restrooms, and a picnic and swimming area, open seasonally. Boating access to Parr Reservoir on the Broad River is provided by two boat ramps. To reach them, drive about 12 miles east of Newberry on SC 34. Turn right on S-36-28 and drive about 5 miles to Heller's Creek boat landing. Cannon's Creek landing is another 3 miles south on S-36-28 and offers slightly better viewing opportunities. Finally, to reach the Broad River Waterfowl Management Area from Newberry, stay on SC 34 until it crosses the Broad River, then take the first dirt road on the right. Follow signs to the gate, where you must leave your car and walk.

Extras: For more information, call the DNR's regional office in Union at (864) 427-4771.

Canada geese (Branta canadensis) *have become a familiar sight in South Carolina, due in large part to the DNR's intensive management efforts at Broad River WMA.* Photo by Phillip Jones.

29 Kings Mountain State Park

Where patriots and Tories once fought a decisive battle of the Revolutionary War, you can now enjoy a peaceful hike through woods laced with streams, springs and interesting rock outcrops. Plan to visit the park's living history farm and Kings Mountain National Military Park, which straddles the North Carolina/South Carolina border immediately adjacent to the state park.

As if preventing escape, a split-rail fence at the Living History Farm holds an impressive mass of lance-leaved coreopsis (Coreopsis lancelata). *Photo by Phillip Jones.*

What to look for: On the 16 miles of trails through oak/hickory forest and mixed pine and hardwood forest, watch for scarlet tanagers and pine warblers in summer. At night, listen for the distinctive calls of barred owls and whip-poor-wills. Chipmunks, a visual treat for those who live below the fall line, are plentiful. Although you're not likely to see them, bobcats, gray foxes and flying squirrels also make a home here. Depending on the season, you may see Canada geese, hooded mergansers, wood ducks and buffleheads, as well as herons, on or near the ponds. If you fancy reptiles and amphibians, watch for Eastern box turtles, marbled salamanders and leopard frogs. Timber rattlesnakes may occasionally be seen here, too. For the wildflower enthusiast, the park boasts trilliums, cranefly orchids, galax, atamasco lilies, lycopodium (running cedar) and trees typical of Appalachian cove forests such as Fraser magnolia (umbrella tree) and Carolina silverbell.

When to go: Fall color is wonderful, as are spring wildflowers. From April to September, the park is open from 7 a.m. until 9 p.m. During the remainder of the year, it opens at 8 a.m. and closes at 6 p.m.

How to get there: The park is 14 miles northwest of York on SC 161. Watch for park signs on the left.

Extras: Fishing boats, pedal boats and canoes for rent. Equestrian trail, 119 campsites, primitive facilities for scouts and other groups. Interpretive programs offered; inquire at the entrance gate. Entrance fees charged on a seasonal basis. For information, call (803) 222-3209.

Was Rock Hill a prairie in ancient times? No one knows for sure, but a commonly accepted theory says prairie once covered much of this area of the state. Remnants of that prairie past, including an endangered species of sunflower, are preserved here.

What to look for: Blackjack oaks, which eke out an existence on poor soils, are common here and give the site its name. The preserve was established to protect the federally endangered Schweinitz's sunflower, but it also shelters other representative species of prairie habitat, many of which are found nowhere else in the state. Among the prairie-loving species are prairie dock, three species of liatris, coreopsis and the Carolina rose. Rock outcrops of gabbro make the soil basic and contribute to the unusual plant communities found here. In all, the preserve provides habitat for three rare plant communities and 21 rare plant species. Birds of prey come in search of a meal — perhaps a chipmunk or other small mammal. Look for red-tailed and red-shouldered hawks and great horned, barred and screech owls. Songbirds to excite the birder include the yellow-billed cuckoo, prairie warbler and summer tanager.

When to go: The preserve is open from daylight to dusk. Most of the wild-flowers here bloom in the late summer and fall.

How to get there: From Exit 73 of I-77 south of Rock Hill, take SC 901 to SC 72 by-pass and turn right. Drive approximately 0.25 mile and turn right on Blackmon Road. The preserve entrance is approximately 0.25 mile on the right.

Extras: Rough trail slightly less than a mile long available; more trails planned. In winter, or after heavy rains, trail can be muddy; dress accordingly. For information about this preserve or the state's Heritage Trust Program, call (803) 734-3893.

Blossoms on the large blazing star (Liatris scariosa) *circle stalks as tall as five feet.* Photo by Ted Borg.

31 Landsford Canal State Park

Huge white flowers waving several feet over the rocky shoals of the Catawba River — that's the signature image of this park, where rocky shoals spider lilies put on a spectacular show each May and June. It's also a great place to fish, bird-watch, and learn about the development of canals in South Carolina.

What to look for: This is one of two places in South Carolina to see the rare rocky shoals spider lilies. 3- to 4-inch blooms on stalks 1 to 3 feet tall are big enough to be enjoyed from overlooks along the Catawba River. (But the view is even more spectacular from a canoe!) Don't let the spider lilies cause you to slight the many other wildflowers along the park's trails. Wading birds look for fish hidden in the same shoals that provide a firm purchase for the lilies. Ospreys and hawks soar above the river, and you may see one of the eagles known to nest on park property. Fish can be seen (and caught) in the rocky shoals, and various reptiles and amphibians reside along the banks. Look for spotted and marbled salamanders; cricket, chorus and green treefrogs; brown water snakes; and river cooters, turtles generally found north of the fall line. Otters and muskrats frequent the riverbanks, along with deer and turkeys. Trails lead along the river and past stonework locks that carried cotton barges around the rapids during the canal's brief heyday in the 1820s.

When to go: The lilies generally bloom from mid-May through mid-June. The park is open year-round from 9 a.m. until 6 p.m. Thursday through Monday.

How to get there: From Exit 65 on I-77, travel east on SC 9 for 1.5 miles to the town of Richburg. Turn left on SC 223. When SC 223 dead-ends at US 21, turn left and follow signs to the park.

Extras: Easy access makes this an especially good site for kids. Make time to visit the interpretive center in the old Lock Keeper's house. Call (803) 789-5800 for more information or to inquire about canoe trips and other special events.

Thousands of rocky shoals spider lilies (Hymenocallis occidentalis) *bloom in the Catawba river mid-May through mid-June. Photo by Ted Borg.*

This has long been known as a great spot for anglers — both human and avian. Fish-eating birds congregate here in mind-boggling numbers. One DNR survey found great blue herons numbering in the hundreds.

<u>What to look for:</u> Wading birds like herons and egrets are abundant, especially after the breeding season ends. Birds of prey are well represented, with ospreys being common visitors. Eagles and hawks are also relatively common sights. Bonaparte's gulls can be seen here, along with several species of ducks. The woods and fields around the site are home to a variety of song-birds, with migrants swelling the numbers of the residents during the spring and summer. Reptiles and amphibians are plentiful under rocks and logs.

<u>When to go:</u> Wading birds will be present in greatest numbers in August through April, while April and May are the best months for songbirds.

<u>How to get there:</u> From Exit 34 on I-77 (Ridgeway), take SC 34 to the town of Ridgeway. Turn left on Longtown Road and drive approximately 18 miles, crossing Sawney Creek. At the top of the hill, turn left on Saddle Club Road (watch for the Duke Energy sign) and drive to Wateree Dam Road. Turn left, cross Sawney Creek, and at the sport shop, bear right on Wateree Dam Road. Drive 1 mile to the gravel entrance to the landing and viewing area.

Gangly and clumsy in take-off, the great blue heron (Ardea herodias) *in flight displays all the grace and ease of a ballet dancer.* Photo by Ted Borg.

<u>Extras:</u> CAUTION: The river can rise or fall rapidly with operation of the hydroelectric plant at the dam. For more information call (803) 482-5001.

33 Flat Creek Heritage Preserve and Forty-Acre Rock

Few sites in South Carolina offer the diversity of this one. It boasts unusual geology, many streams, a small waterfall, a large beaver pond and several different forest types. Plants of the sandhills, upland forests and bottomlands often grow within a few yards of each other.

Growing in the preserve's vernal pools at various times are stonecrop (Sedum smallii), black rock moss (Grimmia laevigata), rockwort (Arenaria uniflora) and others.
Photo by Robert Clark.

What to look for: Forty-Acre Rock, owned jointly by The Nature Conservancy and the state, is actually a 14-acre granite flatrock outcrop. Over time, rain dissolved minerals in the rock face and created shallow depressions or pools. These pools, wet only during the spring, support highly specialized plant communities of mosses, lichens, sedum and the endangered pool sprite. The sedum fills pools with tiny red plants topped by white flowers until warmer weather eliminates both the pools and the plants. To get the most of your visit, approach the rock through Flat Creek Heritage Preserve. The trail (about 1.5 miles from the parking lot to Forty-Acre Rock) crosses upland and bottomland hardwood forests and passes a beaver pond, several streams and a small waterfall. Spur trails circle the beaver pond and offer an alternate route to the summit. This is a very rich site for wildflower enthusiasts: trillium, jack-in-the-pulpit and green-and-gold are just a few of the many species growing here. Summer tanagers, warblers, blue-gray gnatcatchers, vireos and woodpeckers will enliven your walk, as will the skinks, fence lizards and tiny frogs scurrying to get out of your way.

When to go: To see Forty-Acre Rock at its best, go in March or early April when the pool vegetation is at its peak. A hike through the preserve will be pleasant at any time of year, with wildflowers in the spring and summer and good fall color.

How to get there: From Lancaster, take SC 903 about 13 miles to its merger with US 601. Follow US 601 north approximately 1.5 miles and turn left on S-29-27 (first road on the left after US 601 crosses Flat Creek). The parking area for the Flat Creek Heritage Preserve Trail is 0.4 mile on the left. If you want to go directly to Forty-Acre Rock, drive about 2 miles on S-29-27 and turn left on Conservancy Road. Follow the road to a gate, park, and walk about 1/4 mile to the rock.

Extras: For a site brochure or information about the state's Heritage Trust Program, call (803) 734-3893.

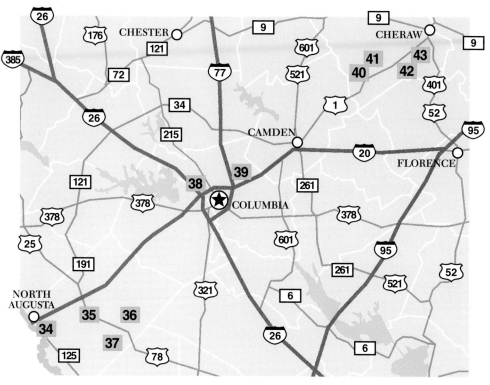

Nature Viewing Sites

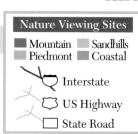

Sandhills

34 Savannah River Bluffs Heritage Preserve

A trail leads from 150-foot-tall bluffs over one of the last remaining shoals on the Savannah River, then along a stream to the riverbank. Along the way, expect beautiful views and a chance to see imperiled rocky shoals spider lilies and other wildflowers. Native Americans may have built funnel-shaped fish weirs out of stone here, accounting for some of the rock formations seen in the river today.

What to look for: Rocky shoals spider lilies turn shallow spots in the river white with their seven-inch blooms in late spring each year, just as they did when noted naturalist William Bartram first saw them here more than 200 years ago. The lilies are now a threatened plant in South Carolina, made rare by impoundments that have eliminated many river shoals. The federally endangered relict trillium, found in only four other places in the country, is among eight rare plants protected here, as are bottle-brush buckeye and upland swamp privet. The preserve includes elements of both coastal plain and piedmont, with the coastal plain's bald cypress and Spanish moss mixing with false rue anemone and yellow-wood, both piedmont plants. Watch for American redstarts, prothonotary warblers, red-eyed vireos and Eastern wood pewees.

When to go: The preserve is open during daylight hours year-round. The lilies are most likely to bloom in late May.

How to get there: Take Exit 1 from I-20, near the Georgia/South Carolina border. After exiting, travel 0.5 mile southeast (toward North Augusta) on SC 230. Turn right on the first road to the right. Drive 0.2 mile and turn right again. Drive 0.3 mile and park in the parking area on the left. Follow the road to the powerline right-of-way, then turn left and follow the right-of-way to the next ridge, where the trail will turn right on an old road.

Extras: For information about this site or the state's Heritage Trust Program, call (803) 734-3893.

Found in only four places in the United States, relict trillium (Trillium reliquum) *grows close to the ground, with distinctly mottled leaves and deep red flowers.*
Photo by Mike Creel.

Called the largest urban forest in the country, this lovely area was donated to the city of Aiken by the Hitchcock family early in this century. Its 2,000 acres are crossed by many paths and trails, all closed to motorized vehicles but available for hikers, horses and horse-drawn carriages.

*Springtime visitors will find the pale pink flowers of mountain laurel (*Kalmia latifolia*) displayed against the plant's dark green, leathery leaves.*
Photo by Ted Borg.

What to look for: This forest contains another precious remnant of the longleaf pine/wiregrass community that used to dominate the Southeast. The woods are crossed by a number of small streams, wetland areas, beaver ponds and a "river of sand" — a unique geological feature that has been the source of folklore and Native American legends. Park at either the Dibble Road or Old Kennels entrance and make your way to Kalmia Trail for a fine display of mountain laurel in late April or early May. This trail, or any of the many others, will also reveal a profusion of wildflowers in spring and summer. The Berric Road or Clark Road entrance will bring you close to Bebbington Springs, an area of natural springs that supports plants more at home in the mountains than in the surrounding sandhills. In drier areas, look for sandhills thistle, lupine, wild rosemary and other plants typical of the sandhills. Many songbirds stop here during migration, joining a rich mixture of residents. Woodpeckers are especially easy to spot.

When to go: The woods are open from sunrise to sunset, year-round. Note posted announcements of equestrian events, and exercise caution.

How to get there: The woods are accessible at different points and most have parking for cars. Main entrance is at Fulmer Stables. From US 1/78 in Aiken. Turn onto Greenwood Road. Turn right onto Dibble Road.

Extras: Map available at each entrance. Exercise caution around horses and carriages. Parking for horse trailers and larger vehicles available at Old Kennels entrance and Fulmer Stables entrance off Dibble Road. For information, call (803) 642-0528.

36 Aiken State Park

Sandhills meet swamp in this 1,067-acre park. A secluded location, four spring-fed ponds, sparkling sandhills streams, and the meandering South Fork of the Edisto River make this an ideal spot for a variety of activities.

Common statewide, monarch butterflies (Danaus plexippus) *are known for their mass migrations. Gathering in the fall, they journey southward to over-winter in the fir forests of Sierra Madre, Mexico.* Photo by *Phillip Jones.*

What to look for: The three-mile nature trail crosses upland vegetation, sandhills streams and wetland areas, while a short loop leads to the river. You'll hear woodpeckers, including the pileated wood-pecker, and see evidence of their work everywhere. Watch and listen for northern parula, prothonotary, Swainson's and pine warblers. Near the water, look for wood ducks, hooded mergansers, pied-billed grebes and wading birds. The river, ponds and moist woods provide excellent habitat for reptiles and amphibians. This is a good spot to look for butterflies, especially mourning cloaks and tiger swallowtails. Big green luna moths are often present, too. Expect to see plants typical of wet, boggy areas like pitcher-plants, red bays and pond pines, as well as typical sandhills vegetation like the spring-blooming lupines. If you want a closer view of the river, arrange to rent a canoe at the park and spend some time on the Edisto River Canoe Trail. It should take between 1.5 and 3 hours to travel this 1.75 mile section of the trail, depending on the energy devoted to paddling!

When to go: The park is open from 9 a.m. until 6 p.m. seven days a week from November through March, and until 9 p.m. from April through October. Spring and fall are best for seeing migrating songbirds.

How to get there: From Aiken, drive 16 miles east on US 78 and follow the signs to the park. The park is also accessible from SC 302. The nature trail begins in the first parking area off the right fork of the park loop road.

Extras: Park has 25 campsites. Public boat ramp where State Park Road crosses the Edisto River. Lake and river fishing available year-round, while pedal boats and lake swimming are available only during the summer. For information, call (803) 649-2857.

The longleaf pine/wiregrass community preserved here is one of the most endangered in the Southeast. Today the DNR conducts summer controlled burns to mimic the lightning fires that used to create ideal habitat for gopher tortoises and the many creatures that share their burrows.

<u>What to look for:</u> Gopher tortoises are the "stars." (For more about these unusual and endangered reptiles, see Tillman Heritage Preserve.) Watch for pine and corn snakes, too, as well as broadhead skinks. This is a good hunting ground for birds of prey; listen for great horned owls, barred owls and red-tailed hawks. Bluebirds, prairie and pine warblers, white-eyed vireos, and brown-headed nuthatches are just a few of the songbirds you may see. Be alert for turkeys and quail.

<u>When to go:</u> "Gophers" will be easiest to spot in the spring. Sandy roads leading to the preserve can be very difficult to navigate in dry weather without a 4WD vehicle.

<u>How to get there:</u> From Aiken, drive south on US 78 for 12 miles to Windsor. Watch for the Aiken State Park sign on the right; approximately 0.5 mile after the park sign, turn left on Spring Branch Road (near the "Lil Country Store"). Drive about 5 miles to the intersection with Oak Ridge Club Road. (Paved Spring Branch Road will become dirt Windsor Road before the crossroads. Oak Ridge Club Road is also a dirt road.) Turn right and drive approximately 1 mile to the preserve, which is on both sides of the road.

<u>Extras:</u> A variety of snakes share gopher tortoise habitat. Keep an eye out for venomous copperheads and timber rattlesnakes. For information about this site or the state's Heritage Trust Program, call (803) 734-3893.

A state endangered species, the gopher tortoise (Gopherus polyphemus) makes its home in underground burrows. Visitors may see these scarce reptiles in the spring, but are cautioned not to disturb them or their habitat. Photo by Ted Borg.

38 Harbison State Forest

Harbison State Forest is called a teaching forest with good reason. Excellent interpretive materials, a location within the Columbia city limits, and an extensive trail and road system crossing its 2,176 acres make this a great place to hike, bike and observe the wildlife typical of South Carolina's Midlands.

What to look for: Upland vegetation near the entrance soon gives way to bottomland hardwoods and riverfront forest near the Broad River. Quail, turkeys and deer live throughout the forest. Birds of prey and neotropical migrants like orioles pass through in the spring and fall, joining many resident songbirds. Coyotes have been seen here, along with foxes, bobcats, fox squirrels and more commonly seen mammals. Near the water, look for salamanders, chorus frogs and treefrogs, turtles and lizards. Tour the forest on the three-mile Stewardship Trail, which can be hiked or biked, or the slightly longer Midlands Mountain Multiple-Use Trail. The former highlights good forestry practices, while the latter winds through a variety of biological communities: pine woodland, bottomland hardwood, river floodplain, slope, cove and field. A short detour brings you to a scenic ridge overlooking the Broad River.

When to go: Forest gates are open seven days a week from 9 a.m. until 4:30 p.m. during the fall and winter, and until 6:30 p.m. in the spring and summer. The best viewing times are early morning and evening. Migratory bird populations peak in spring and fall.

How to get there: Harbison State Forest is located approximately 9 miles northwest of Columbia, on US 176 (Broad River Road) near the inter-section of Interstates 20 and 26. From I-26, take the Harbison Exit and travel north 0.8 mile on Harbison Boulevard until it dead-ends into Broad River Road. Turn right and drive 0.5 mile to the Harbison State Forest entrance sign on the left.

Extras: Trails used extensively by bicyclists, who must purchase a permit. (Contributions are gratefully accepted from hikers, too!) Primitive camping available to organized groups. Trail guides and other materials available. Field trips may be scheduled. Call (803) 896-8890.

The Eastern gray squirrel (Sciurus carolinensis) is able to survive on moisture from dew and plant material, but will use open water if available.
Photo by Phillip Jones.

39 Native Habitat Learning Center
Clemson University Sandhill Research
and Education Center

Few places show off the varied habitats of the Carolina sandhills better than this one, located in the midst of Columbia's expanding suburbs. Nature trails feature three different habitat types: lakeshore, sandhills and hardwood wetlands. This is also one of the few spots in the Midlands where you're likely to see an alligator.

<u>What to look for:</u> Nature trails begin near the Lake House, which is the focal point for a model backyard wildlife habitat. Several alligators patrol the ponds near-by; biologists believe this is near the limit of their natural range. During nesting season, owls, bluebirds, squirrels and many others take advantage of the free lodging provided by a variety of nest boxes. If you follow the one-mile Hard-wood Wetlands Trail, expect wildflowers and a host of birds. Among birds trapped

Very effective hunters, barred owls (Strix varia) *are masters of virtually silent flight.* Photo by Phillip Jones.

and banded by the DNR (which maintains an ongoing program here) are indigo buntings, wood thrushes, summer tanagers, blue-gray gnat-catchers and many more migratory and resident species. Watch along the small woodland streamsand the short Lakeshore Trail for amphibians. At times, the edges of the lake are black with tadpoles! On the half-mile Sandhills Trail, be especially attentive to the native vegetation, a reminder of what was here before centipede lawns.

<u>When to go:</u> Gates are open from dawn to dusk, seven days a week. More birds will be present in the spring and fall.

<u>How to get there:</u> From Columbia, go east on I-20 and take Exit 80, Clemson Road. Turn left and drive approximately 3 miles to the intersection with Two Notch Road. Cross Two Notch and turn right immediately after crossing the railroad tracks. Follow the road to the dead-end, then turn left and follow the road through a gate to the Lake House. Trails begin on the far side of the building, at the bottom of the hill between the ponds.

<u>Extras:</u> Resource materials available for educators. For information call (803) 788-5700. To see more native sandhills habitat, stop at nearby Sesqui-centennial State Park and explore its extensive trail system, take a dip in the lake, or fish.

40 Carolina Sandhills National Wildlife Refuge

These 46,000 acres on the fall line support an incredible array of birds, mammals, reptiles and amphibians, a wildlife bounty all the more remarkable because the land was eroded and barren when the refuge was established in 1939.

<u>What to look for:</u> The refuge has been very successful in providing habitat for the endangered red-cockaded woodpecker. Look for white bands painted on nest-cavity trees and white streaks of sap on tree trunks below cavities. The other seven species of woodpecker found in South Carolina also nest on the refuge. Another endangered animal here is the pine barrens treefrog, which thrives in seepage bogs. These bogs also provide habitat for plants that use insects to supply nitrogen they can't get from the poor soil. Look for sweet, yellow and purpurea pitcher-plants, bladder-worts, butterworts and tiny sundews. In cooler months, the refuge's 30 lakes and ponds are home to ducks and Canada geese. These ponds and associated streams attract wading birds and provide a breeding ground for the 25 species of amphibians known to occur here. The area hosts 41 species of reptiles. Turkeys, deer and quail are drawn to food plots, and resident and migrant songbirds make the refuge a bird-watcher's delight.

<u>When to go:</u> The refuge is open year-round during daylight hours only.

<u>How to get there:</u> The entrance to the refuge is 4 miles northeast of McBee on US 1. To view the refuge by car, take the paved 8-mile Wildlife Drive. For a more intimate view of the refuge, take the 1-mile Woodland Pond Trail, which begins near the refuge entrance, or 2-mile Tate's Trail, which crosses most of the major habitat types on the refuge. Maps at the entrance indicate the many other trails and roads open to visitors.

<u>Extras:</u> Fishing permitted in refuge lakes. Boat landings on several lakes and ponds. Observation towers off Wildlife Drive at Oxpen Lake and near Martins Lake, and a photo blind on Tate's Trail near Martins Lake. For information call (843) 335-8401.

*Patiently waiting to rob his host, a pine barrens tree frog (*Hyla andersoni*) hopes to snag insects attracted to the scent of the insectivorous yellow pitcher-plant (*Sarracenia flava*). Photo by Ted Borg.*

What is now productive forestland and wildlife habitat was once sand on a prehistoric beach. During the Great Depression, the federal government purchased the property from landowners tired of trying to wrest a living from the infertile soil. Now in state ownership, the 46,000-acre Sand Hills State Forest provides a wealth of recreational opportunities, with Sugarloaf Mountain serving as the premier nature viewing area.

<u>What to look for:</u> In spring, blue lupines and other sandhills wildflowers carpet the roadsides and sunny breaks in the tree cover. Several types of

Sugarloaf Mountain is a monadnock, or high hill of sand, capped by sandstone, which rises about 100 feet above its surroundings. Photo by Ted Borg.

pitcher-plants also grow here. Parts of the forest are being restored to longleaf pine/wiregrass communities, while others are managed intensively for wildlife. The endangered red-cockaded woodpecker and pine barrens treefrog both live here. Thirteen fish ponds are open year-round, and the new H. Cooper Black Recreation Area serves as a focal point for sportsmen and equestrians using the forest. A 6.4-mile mountain-bike trail begins across US 1 from the State Forest Head-quarters. The Sugarloaf Mountain Recreation Area offers primitive camping, fishing, picnic shelters and a nature trail. Mountain laurel, pyxie moss and other vegetation here are more typical of the piedmont than the sandhills.

<u>When to go:</u> Practical considerations limit most uses of the forest to daylight hours. Be alert to hunting seasons and dress accordingly.

<u>How to get there:</u> From McBee, drive about 9 miles north on US 1. Turn left on S-13-29 and drive about 3 miles to the entrance on the right. State Forest Headquarters is 9.5 miles north of McBee on US 1. The H. Cooper Black Recreation Area is approximately 18.2 miles north of McBee. Take US 1 to Juniper Junction. Turn right on Society Hill Road (S-13-20) and drive 4.5 miles. Turn right at the recreation area sign (State Forest Road TT19), and follow the gravel road 1.5 miles.

<u>Extras:</u> Campers, cyclists, equestrians and ATV-users must obtain a use permit from forest headquarters (open 8:30 a.m. to noon and 1 p.m. to 4:30 p.m., weekdays) or Cheraw State Park golf course club house. For information call (843) 498-6478. Many roads in the forest are unpaved.

43 Cheraw State Park

Not many visitors to South Carolina's oldest state park suspect that past the golf course and playground lies an incredibly diverse natural area. A hiking trail or canoe trip will take you to the cypress swamp headwaters of Lake Juniper, the 300-acre centerpiece of the park.

What to look for: As you walk the nature trails, watch for a redheaded or pileated woodpecker in the oak and longleaf pine forest. Even the endangered red-cockaded woodpecker makes a home here. Upland forest soon turns to cypress swamp, unusual for this part of the state. A popular waterfowl nesting area, it also attracts numerous other birds. Look for wading birds and migrating songbirds. Many raptors — bald eagles, ospreys, red-tailed hawks, northern harriers and Mississippi kites — take advantage of the abundant prey. This is a great place to look for reptiles and amphibians of both the uplands and the coastal plain. You may see Eastern five-lined and ground skinks, banded water snakes, yellow-bellied sliders and painted turtles, and even the endangered pine barrens treefrog. Butterflies include the zebra and spicebush swallowtails. Wildflower enthusiasts will appreciate native irises, called blue flags, in spring and rose pogonia orchids in summer.

When to go: The park is open from 6 a.m. until 9 p.m. from April to October, and from 7 a.m. until 7 p.m. during the remainder of the year. Spring and fall are the best viewing times.

How to get there: Drive about 4 miles south of Cheraw on US 1. Following park signs, bear left on US 52. Entrance is on the right. At the stop sign, turn right and follow the road until it ends. If you are camping or bringing a boat (only canoes or boats with gas engines of 10 HP or less allowed) enter at the second park gate.

On your way up US 1, stop in to see how warm-water fish are produced for stocking around the state. Inside, check out the small aquarium to see the kinds of fish that live in the state's ponds and warmer lakes. Outside, visit the rearing ponds to see young fish. If your visit is between spawning cycles, you may see ducks or other birds searching for tasty leftovers. Most activity occurs at the hatchery between March and November, and you'll find someone to answer your questions during normal working hours. For a guided tour, call (803) 537-7628. The Cheraw Fish Hatchery is approximately 5 miles south of Cheraw.

Extras: Seventeen campsites, 8 cabins and group facilities. Lake fishing. Pedal boat rental in summer. For information, call (843) 537-2215.

This shellcracker (Lepomis microlophus) is one of the six warm-water species reared at Cheraw Fish Hatchery. Photo by Phillip Jones.

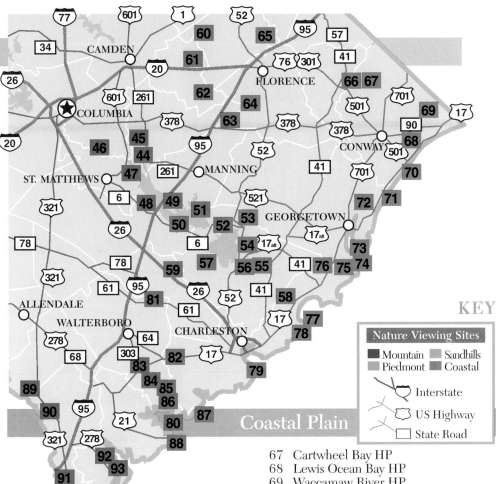

KEY

Nature Viewing Sites

- ■ Mountain
- ■ Piedmont
- ■ Sandhills
- ■ Coastal

- ⬡ Interstate
- ⬡ US Highway
- ▭ State Road

Coastal Plain

44 Poinsett State Park
45 Manchester State Forest
46 Congaree Swamp
47 Upper Santee Swamp
48 Santee State Park
49 Santee National Wildlife Refuge
50 Santee Cooper WMA
51 Bird Island (Lake Marion)
52 Sandy Beach WMA
53 St. Stephen Fish Lift/Bayless Hatchery
54 Lake Moultrie Passage/ Palmetto Trail
55 Wadboo Creek
56 Old Santee Canal State Park
57 Hatchery Wildlife Management Area
58 Francis Marion National Forest
59 Francis Beidler Forest
60 Kalmia Gardens/Segars-McKinnon HP
61 Lee State Park
62 Lynchburg Savanna HP
63 Woods Bay State Park
64 Lynches Scenic River
65 Great Pee Dee River HP
66 Little Pee Dee River HP

67 Cartwheel Bay HP
68 Lewis Ocean Bay HP
69 Waccamaw River HP
70 Myrtle Beach State Park
71 Huntington Beach State Park
72 Samworth WMA
73 Tom Yawkey Wildlife Center
74 Santee Coastal Reserve
75 Santee Delta WMA
76 Hampton Plantation State Park
77 Cape Romain NWR
78 Capers Island Heritage Preserve
79 Fort Johnson-Marine Resources
80 The ACE Basin
81 Edisto River
82 Edisto Nature Trail
83 ACE Basin NWR
84 Donnelley WMA
85 Bear Island WMA
86 ACE Basin NERR
87 Edisto Beach State Park
88 Hunting Island State Park
89 Webb Wildlife Management Area
90 Tillman Sand Ridge HP/WMA
91 Savannah National Wildlife Refuge
92 Victoria Bluff Heritage Preserve
93 Pinckney Island NWR

44 Poinsett State Park

You'll feel like you've traveled South Carolina "from the mountains to the sea" as you explore Poinsett State Park. Hilly terrain and mountain laurel mark the entrance, but as the road drops toward the park headquarters, the hardwoods give way to bald cypress draped in Spanish moss. Several plant species found here are "disjunct" — separated from the rest of their range by a considerable distance.

<u>What to look for:</u> For a sample of "foothills" here in the Midlands, head to the overlook. More typical Midlands vegetation borders the Coquina Nature Trail, named for the building material once mined nearby. The trail begins at the nature center and loops through woods around Old Levi Mill Lake. Remnants of the mill, which predates the Revolutionary War, can be seen near the beginning of the trail. Watch for signs of wild turkeys and deer in the upland areas, and for turtles, mallards and ring-necked and wood ducks in the pond. Egrets and great and little blue herons may be searching the edges of the pond for their next meal. The diversity of the park attracts many different kinds of songbirds, including vireos and warblers so bold they've been seen drinking from campsite spigots. One of the prettiest spots is Christmas Mill Pond, just outside the park gates within Manchester State Forest. In spring, the pond teems with butterflies, frogs, turtles and dragonflies.

<u>When to go:</u> The park is open from 9 a.m. until 6 p.m. from November to March, and until 9 p.m. April through October. The Nature Center is open on Saturdays and Sundays from 1 p.m. until 4 p.m.

<u>How to get there:</u> From US 76/378 near Stateburg, turn south on SC 261. Follow SC 261 for approximately 10 miles. Turn right at the Poinsett State Park sign and follow the road to the parking area.

<u>Extras:</u> Equestrian campsites, 50 regular campsites and 4 cabins. Year-round fishing. From May through October, rent a fishing boat, pedal boat or swim in the lake. Park's 6-mile equestrian trail connects to 25 miles of equestrian trails on Manchester State Forest. Parking fee. Call (803) 494-8177 for information.

Coquina is a coarse form of limestone. Shell fragments accumulated and cemented together thousands of years ago, when the Atlantic Ocean covered the area now known as Poinsett State Park. Photo by Phillip Jones.

Equestrians, mountain bikers, hikers and motorcyclists
now flock to this forest, once the site of summer estates built by
owners eager to escape the heat and mosquitos of their Lowcountry
riverside plantations. The forest includes mountain laurel, red cedars,
dogwoods and longleaf pines — a plant mix unique in the state.

What to look for: Within the 23,500 acres of the forest are ridges, sandhills,
hardwood bottomland, ponds, cypress swamps and wetlands. Bird-watchers
will delight in an array of songbirds, wading birds and birds of prey. The
endangered red-cockaded woodpecker also makes a home here. Near
ponds and wetlands, look for butterflies and dragonflies, turtles,
salamanders, frogs, snakes, lizards and alligators. Separate trails are
maintained for horses, mountain bikes, motorcycles and hikers. If you're
looking for a short hike,
try the nature trail
around Campbell's
Pond, near the forest
headquarters.

*Their ability to climb trees may be one reason that
gray foxes (Urocyon cinereoaregenteus) have not been
displaced by coyotes, as have many red foxes.
Photo by Phillip Jones.*

When to go: Bird-watching
will be best in spring
and fall. Because most
areas of the forest are
open to hunting, be sure
to wear brightly colored
clothing during hunting
seasons. The forest trails
are open year-round
during daylight hours.
The headquarters
building, where permits
must be obtained, is
open from 8 a.m. until 5
p.m. Monday through
Friday.

How to get there: From US 76/378 near Stateburg, turn south on SC 261.
Drive about 9 miles and turn right at the State Forest Headquarters
sign.

Extras: Only electric motors allowed on the four forest ponds, available for
fishing year round. Groups larger than 15 should check in at the headquarters. Weekend use by organized groups during spring and fall is so
heavy that it may be helpful to call ahead before planning an outing.
Permit required for trail users except hikers. For information call (803)
494-8196.

46 Congaree Swamp National Monument

On a spring weekend, you're as likely to meet someone from Germany, Colorado or California in "the Congaree" as you are to meet a fellow South Carolinian. People come from around the world to marvel at this remnant of old-growth riverbottom hardwood forest, now protected by the National Park Service and designated as a part of the international Man and the Biosphere Program to preserve genetic diversity and act as an indicator of our planet's overall health.

What to look for: The number of tree species found here equals half the number found in all of Europe. Many are the largest of their species, despite losses sustained during Hurricane Hugo. All eight species of woodpecker found in the Southeast this their home. More than 30 species of warblers have been seen here. You may also see flycatchers, wading birds, bald eagles and Mississippi kites. This is a great place to look for snakes, salamanders and frogs. Watch for river otters, too. If you see hoof prints, they were probably made by deer or by feral (wild) hogs. Miles of well-marked trails cross the Monument, but most first-time visitors take the wheelchair-accessible boardwalk that leads to Weston Lake. A trail guide is available at the Ranger Station.

Zebra longwing butterflies (Heliconius chariyonius) *gather to roost in groups each night. The larval stage, a white caterpillar with black spines, feeds on passion flowers.* Photo by Phillip Jones.

When to go: Fall, winter and spring are the best times to see wildlife, but those champion trees are there in the summer, too! In wet weather (generally December - April) parts of some trails and the lower boardwalk may be flooded. The park gates are open from 8:30 a.m. until 5 p.m., but you can stay until dark if you park your car outside the gates.

How to get there: Take Exit 5 (Bluff Road) on I-77 south of Columbia, and travel approximately 8 miles southeast toward Gadsden. Following the sign, bear right on Old Bluff Rd. and drive an additional 4.6 miles. At the sign, turn right and drive 1 mile to the Ranger Station.

Extras: For information call (803) 776-4396. Fishing allowed in Wise Lake and Cedar Creek with a South Carolina fishing license. Primitive camping by permit only.

These 16,000 acres of swamp blur the dividing line between the Santee River and Lake Marion. If you have access to a small boat, you can see some of the most interesting swampland in the state.

<u>What to look for:</u> One of the most striking things about this swamp is the prevalence of small hummocks of cypress trees. If (and only if) you have a good navigational chart, wind your way through the many small creeks to Indigo Flats, considered by many to be one of the most beautiful areas in Upper Santee Swamp. The swamp hides the largest nesting colony of great blue herons in the state. In spring and fall, the swamp is filled with migrating songbirds, while colder months bring abundant waterfowl. Moving quietly, you might see turtles, snakes, or even an alligator. Many people come here to fish. Bass, catfish and bream are plentiful. The woods near Low Falls Landing are typical of mature upper coastal plain hardwoods and hide native woodland plants like wild ginger, dwarf red buckeye and deciduous azaleas.

<u>When to go:</u> Spring and fall are the best times for bird-watching, while winter is the best time to observe waterfowl (but be aware of hunting seasons.). Nearby public boat landings are open all year, and there are no restrictions on travel in the swamp.

Beautiful and deceptively serene, this section of Lake Marion is facing the danger of being choked by agressive aquatic plants. Photo by Phillip Jones.

How to get there: If you're on Lake Marion, simply head north. To reach Low Falls Landing on the west side of the lake, drive 1 mile northwest of Elloree on SC 6. Turn right (northeast) on SC 267 and drive approximately 4.5 miles. Turn right on S-9-286 and drive approximately 3 miles to Low Falls Landing. To reach upper Lake Marion from the east side of the lake, use the Sparkleberry or Rimini public landings, located off S-43-51 near Rimini.

Extras: Many of the beautiful flowers you'll see blooming in the water belong to nuisance aquatic weeds like alligator weed and water hyacinth. Clean your boat, propeller and trailer carefully to avoid transporting weeds to another water body. For more information call Santee Cooper Property Management Division at (843) 761-4068.

48 Santee State Park

Head to Santee State Park if you want to enjoy Lake Marion but don't want to settle for just one pursuit. Within its 2,496 acres, you can boat, fish, swim, hike or bike on a nature trail or see rare sinkholes and caverns.

<u>What to look for:</u> The centerpiece of the park is the lakefront, where you can see wading birds and shorebirds, as well as ospreys and an occasional eagle. Like humans, they come to the Santee Cooper lakes to fish. The Visitor Center offers information about the cultural and natural history of the area, and nature trails remind you that there's more to the park than the lake. Walk the 1-mile Limestone Nature Trail or the 0.4-mile Sinkhole Pond Trail for a look at the sinkholes, which give a hint of the caverns in their geologic infancy on the site. This area of karst topography (the name given to such limestone dominated areas) is home to the rare Southeastern myotis bat and several rare plant species, along with salamanders, frogs, crayfish, and a host of songbirds. Wildlife food plots within the park attract wild turkeys, deer and other animals.

<u>When to go:</u> The park is open from 6 a.m. until 10 p.m. daily, while the Visitor Center hours are 8 a.m. to 6 p.m. Summer is the only time you can take advantage of the protected swimming area or rent pedal boats. Bird-watching will generally be best in spring and fall, but you're more likely to see wild turkeys in winter.

<u>How to get there:</u> Take Exit 98 from I-95 or Exit 154 (US 301) from I-26 and follow signs to the park. The park is located just off SC 6, about 3 miles northwest of the town of Santee.

<u>Extras;</u> A 6.8-mile bicycle trail, 174 campsites in two lakefront camping areas, and 30 fully equipped cabins, 10 of which hover over the lake on piers. Other conveniences: restaurant, open for three meals daily, Thursday through Sunday, store/tackle shop and a meeting facility available for rent. Two cabins and some additional facilities are wheelchair-accessible. Rent fishing boats at the park but bring your own gas motor. For information, call (803) 854-2408.

A limestone cavern, replete with carved evidence of earlier visitors. The soft material is fragile; explorers are encouraged not to touch.
Photo by Phillip Jones.

Interstate 95 makes this a **convenient** spot to see a slice of everything you're likely to find along the shores of the Santee Cooper lakes. The refuge's 15,095 acres include lake shore, ponds, wetlands, diverse upland areas and remnants of the area's historic and prehistoric past.

Blast off! Blue-winged teal (Anas discors) *are one of nearly 20 duck species wintering at the refuge.* Photo by Robert Clark.

What to look for: Begin with an overview of the site at the Visitor Center, then drive a half-mile to the parking area. Take time to see the site of Fort Watson, a Revolutionary War-era fort built on top of the Santee Indian Mound, the remnant of a temple dating to 1000 A.D. The 1-mile Wright's Bluff Nature Trail is a quick way to see some of what the NWR has to offer. Look for quail in the upland areas, songbirds in the forest and wading birds in the wetlands. Near the lake shore, you're likely to see killdeer and ospreys. During the winter months, tundra swans, Canada geese, and as many as 20 species of ducks settle in. Several observation points make it possible to view waterfowl when many areas of the refuge are closed. For a panoramic view of the refuge, go to the entrance gate of the Cuddo Unit on SC 260 and take the Visitor Drive. The drive has several loops and offers access to two different 1.4- mile foot trails. A map is available at the Visitor Center.

When to go: Most refuge areas are open for hiking or biking between March and October, but closed the rest of the year to avoid disturbing wintering waterfowl. The Visitor Center is open Monday through Friday from 8 a.m. to 4 p.m., while the nature trail is open from 8 a.m. until 6 p.m. October through March and from 7 a.m. until 7 p.m the remainder of the year. Wintering waterfowl are most plentiful from November to February, while April and September are the best times to look for migrating songbirds.

How to get there: From I-95, take Exit 102 (first exit on the east side of Lake Marion) and follow signs to Santee NWR.

Extras: Visitor Center overlooking the lake is wheelchair accessible. Nearby public boat landings include John C. Land off SC 261 and Taw Caw Creek Park. For information call (803) 478-2217.

50 Santee Cooper Wildlife Management Area

While you won't see all **3,144 acres** of the WMA from the 1.4-mile nature trail, you will see enough to whet your appetite for longer excursions. Limestone sinks, depressions of one to three acres, dot the WMA and hold water during all but the most extreme droughts.

What to look for: The WMA includes about 850 acres of shallow water cypress flats, an excellent nursery for many lake inhabitants. Wading birds seem to know that too! Expect to see egrets, herons, including the tri-colored heron, and bitterns. Watch the sky for hawks, owls, bald eagles and an occasional golden eagle. The earlier you visit in spring, the more waterfowl you're likely to see, including Canada geese, gadwalls, wigeons, ring-necked ducks, mallards and wood ducks. Be on the lookout for deer, wild turkeys and river otters. The limestone depressions are good places to spy reptiles and amphibians. In general, the habitat here is typical of the upper coastal plain of South Carolina.

When to go: The Nature-Education trail is open to the public during daylight hours from March 2 through August 31. Santee Cooper WMA is closed to all public access from October 20 until March 1 except for special hunts designated by the DNR.

How to get there: From Eutawville, travel 2.5 miles northeast on SC 6. Turn left onto S-38-137 and drive 1.2 miles. The parking lot for the Nature-Education Trail is on the left.

Extras: Trail includes some boardwalks and observation platforms. Suitable for wheelchairs and strollers except in very wet weather. Signs describe wildlife and forestry management practices. Both the WMA and nature trail are closed until noon every Saturday morning in April. Call (843) 825-3387 for information.

Sound wildlife management, environmental clean-up and wetlands protection have helped restore a good population of river otters (Lutra canadensis) to all areas of the state. Photo by Phillip Jones.

Bird Island is accessible only by boat, but it is worth the effort to see the largest wading bird colony in the state.

White ibises (Eudocimus albus) *feed noisily in shallow water and muddy sloughs. They wade back and forth, thrashing the water with their down-curved beaks partially submerged.* Photo by Phillip Jones.

What to look for:

As you view the island from a safe distance, look for wading birds tending their nests. The island is heavily used by white ibises, cattle and great egrets, little blue, black-crowned night, and tri-colored herons and anhingas. At times, more than 2,000 great egret nests have been built on the island, defying predictions made by noted ornithologists at the turn of the century that wading birds like the egret would become extinct within decades. As the birds fly to and from the island, you'll see that individual species come from and go to different locations, depending on their feeding preferences.

When to go:

Survival of nesting birds and their young can be jeopardized by any human interference. Anyone who goes on the island between March 1 and August 31 *will be subject to prosecution.* However, you can view the island from a distance of 100 meters (about 300 feet) year-round. The greatest bird concentrations generally occur between May and August.

How to get there:

The closest landings are at Canal Lakes Resort or Hills Landing on the Diversion Canal. To reach the Diversion Canal, drive approximately 19 miles west of Moncks Corner on SC 6. Turn north on SC 45 and drive 2.5 miles to the Diversion Canal. Once in the water, travel northwest approximately 4 miles to Channel Marker 39. Bird Island will be approximately 200-300 yards to your left. Another nearby access point is Harry's Fish Camp on Lake Marion. Expect to pay a fee at any of these access points.

Extras:

For information about the site call the Santee Cooper Property Management Division at (843) 761-4068. For information about the state's Heritage Trust Program call (803) 734-3893. You may also be able to rent a small boat at Rocks Pond or Harry's Fish Camp. Commercial tours available.

52 Sandy Beach Wildlife Management Area

Several loops of the Palmetto Trail pass through this diverse mixture of pine, bottomland hardwood forests and freshwater marsh. Waterfowl come first, however, and the area is closed to vehicles.

<u>What to look for:</u> In the upland areas, you may see deer, turkeys and quail. Waterfowl in residence include Canada geese, mallards, wigeons, teal, gadwalls, ring-necked ducks and wood ducks, South Carolina's only native duck. Wading birds like the same conditions as ducks, so expect to see great blue, little blue, green, and tri-colored herons, ibises, egrets and American bitterns. Birds of prey frequenting the site include bald eagles, ospreys, hawks and owls. If you have sharp eyes, you may catch sight of a river otter, bobcat or coyote. And of course, wetlands make great places to look for alligators, salamanders, frogs, and other amphibians and reptiles.

<u>When to go:</u> The area, including the loop trails, is closed to the general public between November 16 and March 1. Hiking, photography and wildlife observation are permitted from March 2 through November 15. The earlier you visit in March, the more waterfowl you're likely to see. Spring and fall are the best times to observe migratory songbirds.

<u>How to get there:</u> From St. Stephen, travel west on SC 45 for approximately 8.5 miles. Turn left on Sandy Beach Road and continue until you cross the dike. The parking area will be 0.25 mile farther.

<u>Extras:</u> Palmetto Trail system loops total 6.2 miles and offer views of the lake, an eagle's nest and the heart of the waterfowl management area. Two primitive campsites available when trails are open. All visitors are encouraged to wear international blaze orange caps or vests during hunting season — August 15 through January 1. Call (843) 825-3387 for information.

Elegant beauty was almost their demise — fashion elite demanded their long feathers – but since snowy egrets (Egretta thula) *gained protected status, their numbers have rebounded.* Photo by Phillip Jones.

Birds and fish together put on quite a show here, where technology is used to meet both human and animal needs.

DNR employees teach groups touring the facility in-depth information about striped bass (Morone saxatilis). *They also impart information about the white bass and hybrids raised there.* Photo by Phillip Jones.

<u>What to look for:</u> Fish, of course. The hatchery grows them, and the lift allows them to bypass the dam and follow their ancient migration routes into lakes Moultrie and Marion. As many as several thousand fish a day pass by the underwater viewing windows of the lift during the height of migration. These fish are anadromous, spending most of their lives in salt water but returning to freshwater rivers to spawn. The lift allows them to get to their spawning areas which were blocked off by the dam. At the hatchery, see how the DNR ensures large populations of striped bass, white bass and hybrids for the state's lake systems. Birds put on an unexpected "sideshow" at the base of the fish lift, as cormorants, ospreys and eagles swoop and dive for the fish waiting to move upstream. This is a great place to photograph ospreys and an occasional eagle catching fish.

<u>When to go:</u> Water temperature affects migration, but the fish lift is generally open from March 15 to April 15. The powerhouse/fish lift gates are open from 7 a.m. until 7 p.m., and the fish are "lifted" every hour on the hour. An interpreter is often available with a video, information sheets and answers to questions. The hatchery is open from March 1 until the first or second week in May. During peak spawning time, informational tours are presented at the hatchery every hour on the half hour, in coordination with fish lift operation.

<u>How to get there:</u> To reach the fish lift, drive 1 mile northwest of the town of St. Stephen on US 52 to Powerhouse Road. Turn right on Powerhouse Road and follow it to the parking lot. Follow signs to the fish lift viewing area. The hatchery is across the dam; walk if you're already at the fish lift, or drive by returning to US 52 and traveling approximately 1 mile northwest. Turn right at the first road after the rediversion canal, turn right at the "T" dead end, then take the next left. The hatchery is on the right.

<u>Extras:</u> Call (843) 825-3387 for information or to arrange group tours. A nature trail leads along the canal from the parking lot.

54 Lake Moultrie Passage/Palmetto Trail

Thirty-three miles of easy hiking trails provide great views of the lake, resident wildlife and wildflowers. Hike or mountain bike all 33 miles, or break the trip into shorter legs. The Lake Moultrie Passage was the first leg of the 300-mile Palmetto Trail to open. When completed, the trail will stretch from McClellanville in the Lowcountry to the Foothills Trail in the Upstate.

What to look for: Deer, wild turkeys, alligators, beavers, muskrats, river otters and a variety of reptiles and amphibians reside here. Wildflowers (and butterflies) will be especially plentiful after a prescribed burn of the forest; if you see remnants of fire in the understory remember that controlled burning prevents wildfires and improves wildlife habitat. Because the trail borders two habitat types, expect to see many songbirds, especially during fall and spring migrations.

Longleaf pine trees (Pinus palustris) *in the "grass" stage are very resistant to fire. To sprout, seeds need the bare, open ground periodic fires can provide.* Photo by Ted Borg.

When to go: Except for the loop trails through the Sandy Beach WMA (see separate listing), the trail is always open. Much of the property crossed by the trail passes through Wildlife Management Areas, where hunting is allowed from mid-August to January 1. Be sure to wear brightly colored clothing during this period.

How to get there: The southern end of the trail begins at the USDA Forest Service's Canal Recreation Area, approximately 5 miles north of Moncks Corner on US 52 near Santee Circle. The Lake Moultrie Passage ends at the Diversion Canal on SC 45, near Santee Cooper's Cross Generating Station. Restrooms, a hand-operated water pump, trail brochures and other interpretive materials are available at the southern trail head. Parking is available at either end of the trail. In addition, vehicular access to the trail is available at the Russellville Boat Landing at the end of Road S-8-204 and at the end of Sandy Beach Road near the Pineville Fire Tower on SC 45.

Extras: Call Santee Cooper at (843) 761-4068 for information. Primitive campsites available at four sites along trail. Bury human waste 6-8 inches deep at least 200 feet from any water source. Horses and motorized vehicles not allowed on trail, and dogs must be on leash at all times.

The boat landing here offers views of beautiful hardwood swamp forest and great fishing at the same time.

<u>What to look for:</u> The banks of Wadboo Creek are shaded by bald cypress and lined with wetland wildflowers in the spring and early summer. Butterflies and dragonflies add extra color. Upstream, look for bottom-land hardwood swamps, while the downstream banks are bordered by abandoned rice fields and freshwater marsh. The creek is suitable for small boats and canoes, but be aware that the water level changes with the tides. You're likely to see wood ducks, great blue and green herons, great egrets, ospreys and red-tailed hawks. Migrating songbirds that visit the area include vireos, warblers and nuthatches. Along the banks, you may see alligators sunning themselves. River otters, beavers and musk-rats make their homes in the creek as well.

<u>When to go:</u> The boat landing is open year-round with no restrictions. Fishing is great all year, and the wildflower season peaks in the spring.

<u>How to get there:</u> From Moncks Corner, take US 52 north approximately 2 miles. Turn right on SC 402 and drive approximately 2 miles to the Rembert C. Dennis Boat Landing on the left.

<u>Extras:</u> For information call (843) 761-4068. Old Santee Canal State Park is nearby.

A female summer tanager (Piranga rubra) *perches high in the forest canopy. Her mate is much more conspicuous, with warm, red plumage.*
Photo by Ted Borg.

56 Old Santee Canal State Park

Old Santee Canal State Park is rich in both cultural and natural history. For the naturalist, one of the most intriguing areas is the marl forest perched above the more typical wetlands. Sugar maples, trilliums and bloodroot grow high on the limestone-based hill, while only steps away ospreys fish over a Southern wild rice marsh stretching along the banks of Biggin Creek.

What to look for: Four miles of well-marked trails and wheelchair-accessible boardwalks allow you to see as much of the park's creeks and wetlands as you choose. Trails lead through Lowcountry swamp, across picturesque Biggin Creek, along the new Tailrace Canal and across the old Santee Canal. An additional 1-mile primitive hiking trail follows the limestone bluff. Great blue herons nest here and are frequently seen in the wetlands. The park shelters many amphibians and reptiles, including greenish rat snakes, Eastern kingsnakes, rainbow snakes, cottonmouth, timber rattlesnakes, which will be hard to find, and yellow-bellied sliders. These big turtles are easy to spot as they sun themselves on logs. In the Visitor Center, study the history of the nation's oldest canal, and its place in the history of canal transportation. The center also houses a living snake exhibit and the cave theater.

When to go: From Memorial Day to Labor Day, the park is open from 9 a.m. to 6 p.m. weekdays and until 7 p.m. on Saturdays and Sundays. During the rest of the year, the park is open 9 a.m. to 5 p.m. seven days a week. The Visitor Center closes at 4:30 p.m. during the winter months and at 5 p.m. in the summer.

Atamasco lilies (Zephyranthes atamasco), *shown above, are also known as Easter lilies. Other wildflowers in the park include Southern red buckeyes, cardinal flowers, swamp asters, bushy asters, butterweeds, Indian pinks and coral honeysuckle.* Photo by Ted Borg.

How to get there: From Moncks Corner, travel northeast on SC 52, following State Park signs to Stony Landing Road which leads to park entrance.

Extras: Check Visitor Center for programs and to rent a canoe. Parking fee. Free tours of Stony Landing Plantation house (circa 1840) arranged at Visitor Center. House can be rented for special events. For information call (843) 899-5200.

It's hard to think of Lakes Marion and Moultrie without thinking about putting a boat in the water. This is a great place to start.

What to look for: The Hatchery WMA includes about 2,400 acres of shallow Lake Moultrie waters — perfect for fishing in the spring and for seeing waterfowl in the winter. Look for Canada geese, wood ducks, mallards, wigeons and teal. Wading birds and shorebirds common to the area include great blue herons, great egrets, killdeer and spotted sandpipers. You can also see laughing, herring and ring-billed gulls. Ospreys, sometimes called fish hawks, circle overhead looking for their next meal. You should see lots of turtles, snakes and lizards, as well as the biggest resident reptiles — alligators. You'll hear plenty of frogs, especially in the spring. If you're lucky, you may spot a salamander hiding under a leaf or log.

When to go: Fishing is best during the spring, while waterfowl watching will be best in the winter. The boat landing is open year-round, but the area is closed to fishing until 1 p.m. on waterfowl hunt dates.

How to get there: From Moncks Corner, take SC 6 west approximately 7.5 miles. Turn right at Hatchery WMA Boat Landing sign.

Extras: For information call (843) 825-3387.

Known as "fish hawk" or "fish eagle," the osprey (Pandion haliaetus) *is found worldwide. In flight it is recognized by a very white underside and the distinct angle at the "wrist," or bend in its wings.*
Photo by Phillip Jones.

58 Francis Marion National Forest

Named after the famous Revolutionary War hero Francis Marion, who made this area his base of operation, the forest hides a multitude of special places, including Hellhole Swamp and Wambaw Swamp, which sheltered the "Swamp Fox" from the British more than 250 years ago. They're much easier to reach now, and definitely worth a visit.

<u>What to look for:</u> There are examples of just about every coastal plain animal and plant somewhere within the Francis Marion National Forest's 250,000 acres. Visit some or all of these interesting destinations. *I'on Swamp*: Travel north from Charleston on US 17, turning left on Forest Service Road 228 (I'on Swamp Road). Follow a 2-mile nature trail around a former rice field to see species common to bottomland swamps. *Little Hellhole Reservoir:* This 18-acre impoundment surrounded by mature pine forest is located near the Witherbee Ranger District Office. Travel toward Moncks Corner on SC 171, and take the first gravel road to the right (Forest Service Road 258). Red-cockaded woodpeckers, Bachman's sparrows and brown-headed nuthatches make the mature pines home, while wood ducks and wading birds live in the reservoir. *Wambaw Creek Wilderness Area:* From McClellanville, take SC 45 north and turn right on Forest Service Road 211 (Mill Branch Road). Still Landing off Mill Branch Road provides boat access to the Wilderness Area. The huge trees along the creek shelter many types of birds, including black-throated green warblers. As you leave the area, drive north on SC 45 toward Honey Hill and turn left on Halfway Creek Road. The 10-mile stretch of road is an old dune line, now covered in longleaf pines interspersed with hardwood drains, Carolina bays and pocosins. It's a great place for reptiles and amphibians, and also shelters black bears, rare in the Lowcountry. This sand ridge/longleaf pine community harbors several colonies of endangered red-cockaded woodpeckers. *Hellhole Wilderness Area:* Travel north on US 17 from Charleston and turn left on SC 41. Drive about 20 miles to Forest Service Road 158 (Hellhole Road) and turn right. The wilderness area begins about 5 miles down Hellhole

This photograph, taken one and a half years after Hurricane Hugo roared through, shows unmistakable evidence of the storm. Today, many wounds have healed; much new growth has taken place.
Photo by Ted Borg.

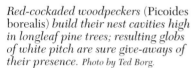

Red-cockaded woodpeckers (Picoides borealis) *build their nest cavities high in longleaf pine trees; resulting globs of white pitch are sure give-aways of their presence.* Photo by Ted Borg.

Road. A canoe trail begins off the main road at the walkway across the water, but is not navigable in dry weather. This is a good place to see endangered wood storks and swallow-tailed kites.

Nicholson Creek Scenic Area: A short trip down Forest Service Road 251-H (Lotti Road) will bring you to the bridge over Nicholson Creek. This area hosts a rare orchid species and two rare species of fern, as well as more typical Southern mixed hardwood forest. Songbirds like prothonotary warblers flourish here. **Santee River Bottomlands:** Reach this forested wetland by traveling north from Jamestown on SC 45 to Forest Service Road 152 (Cooper Ridge Road). Turn right on Cooper Ridge Road and follow it for about 3 miles until it dead ends at an old railroad bed that leads to the river (may be inaccessible during wet seasons). Wild turkeys and deer are abundant here, but the "stars" are warblers: American redstarts, Swainson's, Kentucky and yellow-throated warblers are relatively easy to spot. **North and South Tibwin:** Diverse habitats along the Intracoastal Waterway make this one of the best birding spots in the forest. There is a permanent "hawk station" on Tibwin Creek between North and South Tibwin, where 13 species of raptors may be seen during migrations. Hurricane Hugo's 1989 damage created habitat for painted buntings, yellow-breasted chats and blue grosbeaks. The area is only accessible by foot or bicycle, via access roads leading from US 17 south of McClellanville. **Guilliard Lake Scenic Area:** Turn north onto Forest Service Road 150 from SC 45, about 4 miles south of Jamestown. As you approach the oxbow lake, watch for summer tanagers, Bachman's sparrows and brown-headed nuthatches. Yellow-throated and Northern parula warblers and red-eyed vireos are relatively common here. Watch for swallow-tailed and Mississippi kites. Along Dutart Creek, limestone outcrops support two rare ferns and a plant community unusual in the Lowcountry.

When to go: Migratory birds can be seen during spring and fall; waterfowl viewing is best during winter. Hunting is allowed in many areas of the forest; wear brightly colored clothing during hunting season.

How to get there: Any trip to the forest should begin at the Sewee Visitor and Environmental Education Center on US 17 in Awendaw, about 10 miles north of Mount Pleasant.

Extras: Many camping areas and trails. For information, call (843) 928-3368.

59 Francis Beidler Forest

The beauty, majesty and sheer size of the world's last remaining virgin stand of bald cypress and tupelo gum trees make it easy to see why this 10,500-acre sanctuary is often called a natural cathedral. Walk quietly down the 1.5-mile boardwalk to see a remnant of the great swamp forests that once filled much of the Southern coastal plain.

Dry weather exposes bald cypress' (Taxodium distichum) knobby root "knees" and wide, buttressed trunks, stained black beneath high-water marks. Photo by Robert Clark.

What to look for: Many trees here are at least 1,000 years old. Francis Beidler, the lumberman and conservationist who owned the property until his death in 1924, allowed them to stand, and current owners National Audubon Society and The Nature Conservancy have continued to leave the forest alone. Dead trees rest where they fall, and wildlife comes and goes as it likes. A boardwalk crosses swamp forest that appears as it did when ancient people fished in the surrounding Four Holes Swamp. Prothonotary and parula warblers, great-crested flycatchers, and white-eyed vireos intrigue bird-watchers, while wildflower enthusiasts should look for green-fly orchids, atamasco lilies and dwarf trilliums.

When to go: The sanctuary is open from 9 a.m. until 5 p.m. Tuesday through Sunday. It is closed Mondays, Thanksgiving Day, December 24, 25 and 31, and January 1. The best wildlife and wildflower viewing opportunities occur in the spring, although the forest is awe-inspiring in any season.

How to get there: From Columbia, take Exit 177 on I-26 and follow signs along US 178 and S-18-28 to the sanctuary. From Charleston, take Exit 187 and follow signs along SC 27, US 78, US 178 and S-18-28.

Extras: Admission fee. Canoe trips, night walks, other special events offered in spring and summer by reservation. Naturalist-led group tours can be arranged. The Visitor Center and boardwalk are wheelchair-accessible, and a wheelchair is available. For information call (843) 462-2150.

These sites show two faces of Black Creek. On the 60-foot drop from the bluff to the river, "Miss May" Coker planted a 30-acre garden. The signature plant is mountain laurel, abundant enough in this Pee Dee setting to lend its Latin name, *Kalmia latifolia*, to the gardens themselves. Across the creek is the 796-acre Segars-McKinnon Heritage Preserve, a showcase for vegetation in its natural state.

What to look for: The abundant flowers of the gardens attract an equally abundant butterfly population, and the many habitat types allow a variety of bird species to flourish here. In upland pine groves, look for pine warblers, pine siskins and brown-headed nuthatches. In wet hardwood areas, you may see Acadian flycatchers and prothonotary warblers. The shy yellow-billed cuckoo will be hard to spot, but listen for its resonant *kuk-kuk-kuk* call. In wet areas near Black Creek look for wood ducks, kingfishers, herons and killdeer. A bridge leads from the Rhododendron Trail across Black Creek to the flood plain of the heritage preserve. Near the creek, look for pond and bald cypress, red and sweet bay, titi, clethra and other swamp-loving plants. Upland areas are characterized by a longleaf pine/wiregrass community.

When to go: Mountain laurels bloom in May, and spring will be the best time to view flowers. Migrating birds will be most abundant in the spring and fall. The gardens are open year-round, from dawn until dusk, making early morning birding trips easy.

How to get there: From downtown Hartsville, go 2.6 miles west on SC Business 151 (West Carolina Avenue). The entrance to the gardens will be on the right.

Extras: Extensive interpretive material available, including birding list and listing of trees, shrubs and woody vines on the property. Plans call for trails, including a canoe trail, through the preserve. For information about the gardens, call (843) 383-8145. For information about the preserve or the state's Heritage Trust Program, call (803) 734-3893.

Brilliant, darting sunbeams, prothonotary warblers (Protonotaria citrea) *are fascinating to watch in southern wetlands. They are cavity nesters, lining their nurseries with moss.*
Photo by Phillip Jones.

61 Lee State Park

This park on the banks of the Lynches River is full of unexpected pleasures, including excellent equestrian facilities and a trail through exceptional sandhills habitat.

<u>What to look for:</u> Habitats here range from dry sandhills to the wetlands adjoining the Lynches River, so expect to see a wide variety of plants and animals. A short walk will take you through upland forest, sandhills and bottomland hardwood swamps. As you walk, look (or listen) for warblers and other songbirds, woodpeckers and wild turkeys. When you reach the river, look for wading birds, river otters, beavers and muskrats. If you see a black turtle with yellow or orange spots, it's likely to be a rare spotted turtle. The wetlands where this turtle lives are good places to look for other reptiles and amphibians. Leave your car at the equestrian campground off the loop road and take the Sandhill Trail through the protected Sandhills Natural Area. The detour will reward you with a window into beautiful and fragile sandhills vegetation. To see a completely different habitat type, head toward the community building. Behind a series of small ponds, you'll find swamps teeming with wildlife.

<u>When to go:</u> The park is open from 9 a.m. until 6 p.m. November through March and until 9 p.m. from April through October. Periods of heavy rain may close part of the Loop Road; if river access is important, you may want to call ahead to ensure availability.

<u>How to get there:</u> From Exit 123 near Bishopville on I-20, travel north 1.2 miles to the park entrance.

<u>Extras:</u> Call (803) 428-3833 for information. Park has a fishing pond set aside just for young people. Traditional and equestrian campsites available, and Scout groups may use the designated primitive camping area.

The scarlet kingsnake (Cemophora coccinea) is not venomous and feeds on the eggs of other reptiles. Note the red, black, yellow black pattern. Venomous coral snakes' red and yellow bands are adjacent to each other. Photo by Michael Foster.

The yellow pitcher-plant (Sarracenia flava) *and other insectivorous plants are harbored within this imperiled ecosystem, which is maintained with prescribed burns.* Photo by Robert Clark.

Few people get to see such an excellent example of a wet longleaf pine savanna — listed by botanists and ecologists as one of the most biologically diverse and imperiled ecosystems in North America. It is a haven for unusual and rare plants. In the spring, the mating calls of tiny frogs can be almost deafening.

What to look for: Along the old logging road that loops across the property, look for insectivorous plants such as the yellow pitcher-plant, hooded pitcher-plant and sundew. A rich array of wildflowers, some common and some quite rare, provides color from spring to fall. Lynchburg Savanna has been described as a "hot spot" for a group of sparrow species rarely seen in one place: Bachman's, song, Lincoln's and field sparrows. The older longleaf pines provide nest sites for the endangered red-cockaded woodpecker. Cricket frogs are one of the few frog species active during the day. Although you can't help hearing them, you will rarely see them as they move near the water's edge. In drier areas, look for wild turkeys, bobwhite quail and woodcock.

When to go: The preserve is open from dawn to dusk, seven days a week. Winter is the best time to observe all four sparrow species, while wildflowers will bloom at various times in all seasons but winter. If you're interested in amphibians, visit during late winter or in the spring.

How to get there: From the Bishopville/Elliott exit (120) on I-20, take SC 527 south. Past Elliott, turn left onto S-31-327. The preserve entrance is about two miles on the left. There is a parking area.

Extras: This site is wet! Bring appropriate footwear and drive carefully to avoid getting stuck. Small game hunting allowed. For information about this preserve, or about the state's Heritage Trust Program call (803) 734-3893.

63 Woods Bay State Park

This gem of a park offers a rare glimpse into the heart of a Carolina bay, as well as insights into the social history of the area. Visitors can walk into the bay on a 500-foot boardwalk, explore by canoe, or follow a 0.75-mile nature trail around a millpond — the only remaining evidence of Andrew Wood's grist mill.

A common dragonfly, this little corporal (Ladona deplanata) *rests on Japanese honeysuckle* (Lonicera japonica). *Photo by Ted Borg.*

What to look for: Take the boardwalk to get a close-up view of this magnificent cypress-tupelo community and its inhabitants. Look for anhingas and protho-notary warblers. You may see river otters in the winter and spring. Alligators live in the bay and can be seen in the adjacent Millpond Nature Trail. This trail is also the best spot to look for breeding birds like wood thrushes, blue-gray gnatcatchers, red and white-eyed vireos, orchard orioles, summer tanagers and various warblers. During the spring mating season, the sound of carpenter frogs may remind you of workers nailing boards. The 1,541-acre park includes some of the outer sand rim of the bay as well as evergreen shrub bogs, although neither is easily accessible. These shrub bogs are typical of the vegetation found in an undisturbed Carolina bay.

When to go: The park is open from 9 a.m. to 6 p.m. Thursday through Monday year-round. While there is something of interest during every season, the greatest variety of birds will be present during spring and fall. The Nature Center is open Monday, Thursday and Friday from 11 a.m. until noon and Saturday and Sunday from 9 a.m. to 6 p.m.

How to get there: From Exit 146 on I-95, travel about 7 miles east on SC 341 to S-150 (Norwood Road) or from Turbeville take US 301 to S-48 (Woods Bay Road), following signs to the park. Look for park signs along the way.

Extras: The park rents canoes and loans fishing poles — but bring your own bait! At the Nature Center, see resident species suce as a primitive siren, various snakes and tiny tree frogs. Center is wheelchair accessible. Look for park ranger if Nature Center is locked during operating hours. For a special program, call (843) 659-4445.

What do otters, deep swamps, wood ducks and the site of the state's last duel all have in common? All use (or used) the Lynches River corridor. Beginning just north of Lee State Park and extending downstream to Lynches River State Park is the 54-mile segment of the Lynches River designated as a state Scenic River. To enjoy the river from land, go to one of the two state parks that mark its boundaries. To fully appreciate all that the river has to offer, take a boat and spend some time exploring.

What to look for: As you paddle down the river, look for scenic bluffs, sloughs and artesian springs. Beautiful stands of overcup oak, swamp chestnut oak and river birch line some segments of the river, while stands of cypress occur between US 76 and Lynches River State Park. You'll see herons, hawks, wood ducks, wild turkeys and many song-birds. If you're lucky, you might see river otters, beavers or muskrats. Yellow-bellied sliders may join you in the water.

When to go: Lee and Lynches River state parks are open from 9 a.m. until 6 p.m. November through March and until 9 p.m. April through October. However, during wet weather, part of the Lee State Park loop road with its four river access points may be closed. Public boat landings are always available.

How to get there: The Lynches Scenic River begins at the US 15 road crossing northeast of Bishopville. The boat landing is on the east side of the river. There are additional public boat landings on the west side of US 401, on the west side of US 76, and on the south side of US 52. The entrance to Lee State Park is 1.2 miles north of Exit 123 on I-20 in Lee County. To reach Lynches River State Park drive 12 miles south of Florence on US 52. Turn right (west) at the park sign.

Extras: Camp at Lee State Park. For information, call (803) 428-3833. Lynches River State Park has a swimming pool. For information, call (843) 389-2785. For information about the DNR's Scenic Rivers Program, call (803) 734-9100.

The delicate pink blooms of obedient plant (Physostegia virginianum) *contrast against a Lynches River-bottom backdrop.*
Photo by Robert Clark.

65 Great Pee Dee River Heritage Preserve

This 2,725-acre preserve includes more than seven miles of river frontage and provides habitat for four state threatened species. From the river, it's a boater's delight, while plant enthusiasts will find much on land to interest them.

Although found statewide, bobcat (Felis rufus) *populations are highest in bottomland forests of the coastal plain. These secretive cats may reach 25 pounds or more.* Photo by Ted Borg.

What to look for: Follow the entrance road about 2.3 miles to reach the high bluffs overlooking the Great Pee Dee River. Along the way, look for some of the many wildflowers found in the area. Asters, lilies and orchids provide color during most seasons of the year. River otters and beavers live in the area, as do bobcats, gray foxes, and more common mammals. You'll also see many wading birds, including four species of heron: yellow-crowned night, green, little blue, and great blue. Wood ducks nest in the area, and if you're alert, you may see a wild turkey. This is a great place for birds of prey like ospreys and red-tailed, red-shouldered and broad-winged hawks. As you tour the site, stop to appreciate the beautiful cypress swamp and the river oxbows.

When to go: Wildflowers appear in greatest abundance in the spring, as do migrating songbirds. Fall is also a good time to see migrating birds. The preserve is open during daylight hours, 7 days a week.

How to get there: From Darlington, go 7 miles east on SC 34. As you pass through the village of Mechanicsville, turn left (north) on S-16-35 (North Charleston Road) and drive 1.6 miles. Turn right (east) on marked access road and drive 1.2 miles to the preserve boundary. (The access road passes through private property and trespassing is prohibited.)

Extras: Access road may not be passable in very wet weather. Boat access available nearby at the Cashua Ferry boat ramp, immediately south of the preserve on SC 34, or Blue's boat landing south of Bennettsville in Marlboro County. For information call (803) 734-3893.

Floodplain forests and oxbow lakes characterize the four tracts of this state preserve, which protects about 9,000 acres of forestland and beautiful blackwater river scenery.

<u>What to look for:</u> Otter families play along the river and in the oxbow lakes. Other aquatic creatures to watch for include yellow rat snakes and banded, brown and red-bellied water snakes, all of which are nonpoisonous. Florida and river cooters sun themselves along the banks along with American alligators. You may also see mink, bobcats, gray foxes and raccoons. Many trees here are 80 to 100 years old and provide excellent nesting sites for songbirds. Look for yellow-billed cuckoos, prothonotary warblers, Acadian flycatchers, northern parula warblers, and red- and white-eyed vireos, among others. Upland species such as white-tailed deer, wild turkey and bobwhite quail are common. Several of the preserve's tracts protect the rare sarvis holly. Other rare plants found here include Well's pyxie-moss and Pickering's morning glory. The Ervin Dargan tract provides the best hiking opportunities, while fishing is especially good in the Ervin Dargan and Little Pee Dee tracts.

<u>When to go:</u> The preserve is open from dawn to dusk, seven days a week. Spring and fall are the best times to see birds.

<u>How to get there:</u> The largest area of the preserve, the Ervin Dargan tract, lies on both sides of the river below Galivants Ferry in Horry County. The best access point is Huggins Landing. From the point at which US 501 crosses the river near Galivants Ferry, go east about 0.25 mile to the intersection with Pee Dee Road, turn right and drive 1.3 miles and turn right onto Huggins Landing Road (a dirt road). Follow the road to the boat landing. The preserve lies up- and downstream, and on both sides of the landing. The Little Pee Dee tract is close to the Marion County town of Mullins. From Mullins, drive southeast on SC 917 for 5 miles. After crossing the Little Pee Dee River bridge, turn left at the first entrance road.

Extras: Be careful on dirt roads, especially in wet weather. Paddlers may camp on state property along the banks of the river. For information about this preserve or the state's Heritage Trust Program, call (803) 734-3893.

Odds are good that this cypress (Taxodium sp.) *is providing some wild family a dry home above the tannin-stained waters of the Little Pee Dee.* Photo by Michael Foster.

67 Cartwheel Bay Heritage Preserve
68 Lewis Ocean Bay Heritage Preserve

No one knows for sure how Carolina bays were formed. Nevertheless, scientists value them for their ability to store excess storm water, filter contaminants, and provide habitat for many plant and animal species, some of them endangered. Each of these preserves is actually a complex of bays: the 568-acre Cartwheel Bay Heritage Preserve contains one large 150-acre bay and five smaller ones, while the 9,343-acre Lewis Ocean Bay complex contains 20 undisturbed bays. They offer excellent opportunities to see rare plants and prime songbird and bear habitat.

<u>What to look for:</u> The insectivorous Venus' fly trap is only found naturally in Horry County and in the adjoining coastal plain of North Carolina. You can see it here, on the southern and western rims of the bays. ***Do not break the law by disturbing these plants!*** You can also see pyxie-moss and other plants such as yellow-fringed, white-fringed and rosebud orchids, rose pogonia, pitcher-plants and many other wildflowers, all of which depend on frequent burning of their savanna habitat. While both preserves provide superb birdwatching opportunities, Cartwheel Bay may be the champion. In a single day, veteran bird-watchers spotted 13

warblers: yellow-throated, pine, prairie, black and white, prothonotary, worm-eating, Swainson's, Kentucky, hooded, northern parula, ovenbird, common yellowthroat and yellow-breasted chat. Lewis Ocean Bay Heritage Preserve is known for its pond pine pocosin and longleaf pine sand ridges and excellent black bear habitat. It is also home to the rare savanna milkweed. Many small streams cross the preserve, and during wet weather, the sound of running water mingles with bird calls.

Above: *A delicate, unusual flower, the rosebud orchid* (Cleistes divaricata) *thrives in this environment.* Photo by Ted Borg.
Right: *A bird's-eye view of Lewis Ocean Bay Heritage Preserve clearly shows the bays' elliptical shapes and their raised, sandy rims.* Photo by Phillip Jones.

Carolina bays. . .

. . . are among the most distinctive features of the state's coastal plain. No one knows for sure how they were formed, only that all Carolina bays are shallow, oval depressions oriented in the same direction — north-west to southeast. They range in size from a few to a thousand or more acres. The bays collect rainwater and hold it slightly above the normal water table, creating freshwater wetlands. Some stay wet, while others dry out seasonally. Most support diverse vegetation and wildlife. Typical bays might contain pitcher-plants, bladderworts, vines, grasses, and pond cypress, black gum and bay trees, from which the name is derived.

Extremely rare <u>and protected by law,</u> all Venus' fly traps (Dionaea muscipula) occurring naturally are found in only a few sites in both Carolinas. Many known populations occur in bays. Behind this fly trap is another carnivorous plant, the sundew (Drosera sp.). Photo by Phillip Jones.

When to go: The preserves are open from dawn to dusk. Spring and fall are the best times to see birds. Orchids and other wildflowers bloom from spring through the summer.

How to get there:

Cartwheel Bay Heritage Preserve — From Conway, take US 701 north to its intersection with SC 410. Turn left on SC 410 to the intersection with S-26-19 in Playcard Crossroads. Turn left and continue on S-26-19 for 8.3 miles. Look for the Cartwheel Bay Community Center, a large redwood-colored building, on the right side of the road. Drive an additional 0.2 mile, and turn left between two red houses. (The road looks as though it leads into a farmer's field.)

Lewis Ocean Bay Heritage Preserve — From Conway, drive 1.8 miles southeast (toward Myrtle Beach) on US 501 Business. Turn left (northeast) on SC 90 and drive 7 miles. Turn right to enter the preserve at International Road. A preserve map, available from the DNR, will be very helpful in understanding the bay complex.

Extras: Preserve roads are unpaved and sandy. For information about these preserves or the state's Heritage Trust Program, call (803) 734-3893.

69 Waccamaw River Heritage Preserve

This 5,192-acre preserve provides an excellent wildlife corridor linking black bear habitat in Horry County to larger stretches of bear habitat in North Carolina. If you're extremely lucky, you may see a bear somewhere along the 30 miles of protected river. You'll certainly see beautiful wetlands and bottomland hardwood forests. The Waccamaw River is the only river that originates in a Carolina bay — Lake Waccamaw in North Carolina.

What to look for: River otters, waterfowl and many wading birds enliven a paddle down the river. Look for birds of prey like the Mississippi kite and songbirds, including Acadian and great-crested flycatchers, prothonotary, parula and other warblers, and yellow-billed cuckoos. You're likely to see a pileated woodpecker. The many oxbow lakes in the preserve are home to beavers and mink. Keep an eye out for cottonmouths, but enjoy the harmless snakes and turtles that splash into the water as you approach. The preserve has bald cypress trees, Atlantic white cedar and rare plants.

As if an abstract painting, pondweed (Potamogenton sp.) floats a pattern on ebony and ultramarine water.
Photo by Michael Foster.

When to go: Spring and fall are the best times to see birds, but the scenery may be best in the fall. The preserve is open from dawn to dusk.

How to get there: You can reach the preserve through one of six landings: Red Bluff, Little Savannah Bluff, Big Savannah Bluff, Star Bluff, Horry's Restaurant or Wortham's Ferry. Little Savannah Bluff Landing is marked with a Heritage Preserve sign and can be reached by driving 14 miles northeast of Conway on SC 905 to Red Bluff Crossroads. Continue past the crossroads for 2.1 miles to Watson Carter Road. (First dirt road on the right past Simpson Creek.) Follow Watson Carter Road 1.9 miles to the second dirt road on the right, marked with a Heritage Preserve sign. Little Savannah Bluff Landing is 0.4 mile down this road.

Extras: Paddlers may camp overnight on the riverbank within preserve boundaries; expect to travel 2 mph at low water and 4 mph at high water. Be careful when driving on dirt roads. For more information about this preserve or the state's Heritage Trust Program, call (803) 734-3893.

If you need a respite from the excitement of the Grand Strand, come walk the nature trail and let the wax myrtles remind you how the area got its name. In this 312-acre park, you can swim in the surf, fish from a pier, watch for dolphins or pelicans offshore and spend a pleasant 45 minutes hiking through a remnant of the maritime forest that used to cover much of the area.

What to look for: In the spring, the woods are full of songbirds like summer tanagers, orchard orioles, indigo buntings and various warblers. In the wetlands of the maritime forest, watch for wading birds like green and great blue herons, American egrets and white ibises flying overhead. The nature trail includes a boardwalk over a wetland — a good place to look for reptiles and amphibians. The woods are full of skinks and other lizards, marbled salamanders, box turtles and various snakes. Many wildflowers bloom in the spring, including atamasco lilies. On the shore, you'll see least and sandwich terns, laughing gulls, brown pelicans and cormorants. Look for bottlenosed dolphins offshore. The park naturalist has seen several humpback whales offshore; take your binoculars to the fishing pier and maybe you can, too. Beginning in May, loggerhead sea turtles come ashore to lay their eggs. *It is against state and federal laws to disturb turtles, nests or hatchlings.*

When to go: The park is open from 6 a.m. until 10 p.m. It can be crowded in summer, but summer and fall are the best times to fish or crab from the pier. Summer is also loggerhead turtle nesting season. Spring and fall are the best times to see migrating songbirds.

How to get there: Park is 3 miles south of Myrtle Beach on US 17 Business.

Extras: Park has nature center and a variety of programs (fee charged for some.) Call (843) 238-5325 for information. Amenities include showers to wash the sand off after a stay on the beach, snack bar and gift shop, plenty of restrooms, picnic shelters, camp sites and cabins.

South Carolina's sand dunes help protect our coastal lands from erosion. Several native plants are used to protect the fragile dunes, sea oats (Uniola paniculata) being one of the most often recognized.
Photo by Phillip Jones.

71 Huntington Beach State Park

Many superlatives are used to describe the park, including "best preserved beach on the Grand Strand" and "one of the best bird-watching sites along the East Coast." Sculptor Anna Hyatt Huntington and her husband purchased the area in 1930, leaving both their name and their winter home, the castle-like Atalaya, on the property.

What to look for: The park's 2,500 acres include maritime forest, salt marshes, freshwater ponds and splendid beaches. Serious bird-watchers should note that unusual sightings here include sandhill crane, roseate spoonbill, magnificent frigatebird and swallow-tailed kite. As you enter the park, you'll cross a freshwater lagoon on the right and a salt marsh on the left. Each has a wheelchair-accessible boardwalk and observation decks, from which a variety of shorebirds, wading birds and waterfowl, including tundra swans, can be seen. Alligators live in both areas. Remember that it is illegal to feed them! Watch for avocets, black-necked stilts and greater yellowlegs. On the beach, look for least and black terns, black-backed and Bonaparte's gulls, piping plovers and logger-head turtles. *It is against state and federal laws to disturb turtles, nests or hatchlings.* The jetty at the northern end of the park is a good spot to look for purple sandpipers,

Moments earlier, these baby logger-head sea turtles (Caretta caretta) broke through their leathery egg casings and dug out of the sandy nest in which their mother had placed them two months before. Photo by Phillip Jones.

common eiders, black guillemots, and old squaw and harlequin ducks. The Sandpiper Pond Nature Trail begins near the saltmarsh boardwalk and leads through maritime forest to the beach. It's a great place to look for migrating songbirds.

When to go: The park is open from 6 a.m. until 10 p.m. April through October and until 6 p.m. during the off season. Spring and fall are the best times to see migratory songbirds, while more ducks will be seen in winter. Migratory shorebirds are present in fall, winter and spring.

How to get there: The park is 3 miles south of Murrells Inlet on US 17.

Extras: Interpretive programs offered daily. Check the schedule at the park entrance for exact times and locations, or call (843) 237-4440 for information. Park has 184 campsites. Tours of Atalaya offered during the summer for a small additional fee. Entrance fee charged.

When Thomas Samworth left his beloved Dirleton Plantation to the people of the state, he left us magnificent views of the Pee Dee and Waccamaw rivers, marshes, managed wetlands rich with wildlife, and extraordinary hunting and fishing opportunities.

What to look for: If you have access to a boat, travel upstream about 10 minutes from the WMA headquarters to the wildlife observation tower on Butler Creek. Look for otters and beavers, as well as land mammals such as bobcats and red and gray foxes. Expect to see a variety of shore-birds and wading birds, including yellow-crowned night herons, dunlins, and king, Virginia and sora rails. Several species of ducks reside here in winter while birds of prey patrol the air year-round. You can see most, if not all, of the same species from the banks of the river or from the 1.5-mile nature trail that passes along the river, skirts a small ricefield reserve and crosses open fields and woods. In the spring and fall, the woods are a good place to look for warblers, sparrows, gnatcatchers and many other songbirds.

When to go: The WMA is open during daylight hours seven days a week. Spring and fall are the best times to see migratory songbirds, while ducks will be more common in late fall and winter. Early morning is the best time for bird-watching. Visitation is restricted during annual waterfowl hunts; call ahead to ensure availability.

How to get there: From Georgetown, drive about 6 miles north on US 701. After crossing the Black River, turn right (east) onto S-22-4 and drive 3 miles; the road will turn sharply to the left and become S-22-52. Drive an additional 3 miles to the entrance sign on the right. WMA head-quarters and parking will be about 1 mile ahead on the dirt road.

Extras: For information, telephone (843) 546-9489. Fishing allowed in the managed wetlands and aban-doned rice fields from March 15 until August 31. Boat landing at WMA headquarters.

Easy to recognize, wood duck (Aix sponsa) *drakes are more colorful than hens. Efforts in recent years to increase woodies' numbers have been very successful. Photo by Ted Borg.*

73 Tom Yawkey Wildlife Center

Considered one of the most outstanding gifts to wildlife conservation in North America, the three islands that constitute the Tom Yawkey Wildlife Center were willed to the state in 1976 by the late Tom Yawkey, owner of the Boston Red Sox. A Yale graduate, avid outdoorsman and self-taught ornithologist, Yawkey established sound, innovative management practices that continue today. Once a hunting preserve, the 20,000-acre property is now a premier nature preserve and research center.

Wood storks (Mycteria americana) *are large, elegant white birds with black flight feathers. Often called Flintheads, these birds are becoming more common in the state. Photo by Ted Borg.*

What to look for: Since all visits to the center are by reservation only and guided by DNR personnel, you are ensured an educational field trip. The diverse habitats support large numbers and varieties of waterfowl, wading birds, shorebirds, nesting eagles and other wintering raptors. Depending on the season, you may see rafts of waterfowl resting on former rice fields or thousands of migrating shorebirds and wading birds dining on the smorgasbord left as the water levels are lowered in the spring. On higher ground, wild turkeys and deer move about fearlessly. Your guide may point out nest cavities of endangered red-cockaded woodpeckers in older longleaf pines, and you may be able to glimpse the birds themselves. Endangered wood storks have been known to populate the center in summer, and in the winter American avocets, fairly rare to the East Coast, are found here. Large number of loggerhead sea turtles nest on the beaches of North and South islands. North Island is a true wilderness, only accessible by boat. Local vendors offer excursions to the beachfront. Call the Georgetown Chamber of Commerce at (800) 777-7705.

When to go: Visitors may only tour the center on pre-arranged weekly field trips guided by DNR staff. Educational field trips last three hours, and should be scheduled at least three months in advance. Trips accommodate 14 people and are offered on Tuesday afternoons year-round.

How to get there: The Tom Yawkey Wildlife Center is located 10 miles southeast of Georgetown. Details are provided with reservations.

Extras: For information, or to schedule a field trip, call (843) 546-6814 or write: Yawkey Wildlife Center, One Yawkey Way South, Georgetown, SC 29440.

Hidden within the 24,000 acres of the reserve is the oldest wading bird rookery in continuous use in North America. More visible are the many ducks that flock to the 12,000 acres of impounded wetlands. Extensive trails let you tailor a hike to your interests and energy level.

What to look for: Although the reserve is considered a waterfowl management area, it provides homes for many other birds, including the endangered red-cockaded woodpecker and wood stork. The reserve has one of the largest concentrations of nesting ospreys along the eastern seaboard. More than 300 bird species have been identified here, so be prepared to consult a field guide often. Watch for alligators and for alligator crawls, cleared paths across dikes that indicate frequent crossing spots. Otters,

Ospreys (Pandion haliaetus) *build nests of sticks, debris and trash high atop posts or dead trees. These birds are specially equipped to catch fish. They have vision that corrects the water's refraction, and feet that grip with raised, spiked scales.*
Photo by Phillip Jones.

beavers, deer, bobcats and other mammals live in the reserve. Keep an eye open for wildflowers, including blue flag, atamasco lily and patches of hooded pitcher-plants in bloom.

When to go: The reserve is open from 1 p.m. to 5 p.m. during February. From March through October, hours are from 8 a.m. to 5 p.m. Monday through Saturday, and 1 p.m. to 5 p.m. Sunday. Visits during the remainder of the year must be arranged with the reserve manager. The best bird-watching is in winter and during April and May.

How to get there: From SC 45 in McClellanville, go north on US 17 about 3 miles to the intersection with South Santee Road. Turn right and follow the road an additional 2.7 miles to Santee Gun Club Road. Turn right and follow that road for 2.7 miles to gates marking the reserve headquarters.

Extras: Primitive camping available with free permit from reserve manager. Fishing permitted at Santee River dock and Hogpen impoundment. Contact the reserve manager at (843) 546-8665 for information. Trails include the 1.1-mile Woodland Trail, the 2.9-mile Marshland Trail, a 7.2-mile bike/hiking trail and a 4.25-canoe trail. (May not be accessible during some seasons because of water level manipulations. Bring your own canoe.) If time or mobility is limited, sample the reserve by parking near the headquarters gate and walking a short distance down the Marshland Trail to the 800-foot boardwalk leading into the Washo Reserve.

75 Santee Delta Wildlife Management Area

Tucked between the North and South Santee rivers, this WMA offers opportunities for wildlife observation and photography, fishing and hunting. It's a great place to see a sampling of South Carolina's coastal marshlands if visiting time is limited.

What to look for: The WMA is managed as waterfowl habitat, so expect to see plenty of ducks in the winter and wading birds throughout the year. Ospreys, hawks and other birds of prey (including bald eagles in the winter) circle the marsh, looking for lunch. In summer, swallow-tailed kites forage across the area. Typical coastal plain mammals share the upland areas and riverbanks with alligators, turtles and a variety of snakes, lizards and salamanders. Watch for differences between the North and South Santee rivers and associated marshes, as this area is a transitional zone between fresh and brackish habitats.

When to go: The entire area is open to the general public from January 21 through October 31, while only a few restricted sites may be visited during daylight hours between November 1 and January 20. Watch for signs indicating availability.

How to get there: The WMA is approximately 10 miles south of Georgetown on US 17 and can be accessed directly from the highway. The Pole Yard Landing is on the northeast side of the North Santee River and provides public access to the WMA from the river.

Extras: Fishing allowed in the managed wetlands from March 15 through August 31. Anglers may walk along the dikes or enter using boats without gasoline motors. For information call (843) 546-9489.

*Delta waters provide
a rich habitat for birds,
alligators and other
wildlife residents.*
Photo by Phillip Jones.

It's a short walk through moss-draped trees from the mansion's porch to the Santee River. *Photo by Robert Clark.*

Nestled between the Francis Marion National Forest and the South Santee River, the park offers a river observation boardwalk, a 3-mile walking trail through interesting wetlands and a glimpse into the area's plantation past.

What to look for: Several rare or endangered species can be found in and around the park, including red-cockaded woodpeckers (look for a sign near the park entrance), swallow-tailed kites, Mississippi kites, wood storks, bald eagles, and Rafinesque's big-eared bats. A walk along the river boardwalk or wetland portions of the nature trail may reveal great blue, green or night herons, as well as white ibises and Virginia rails. Chicken turtles, mole salamanders and Mabee's salamanders, all hard-to-find species typical of pine savannas and bogs, live here. After a heavy rain or in the early evening, you may see the normally nocturnal scarlet and rainbow snakes. Both snakes are harmless, unlike the Eastern diamondback rattlesnake, which also inhabits less-traveled areas of the park. The golden silk spider, indigo grasshopper and zebra swallowtail butterfly are unusual invertebrates found at the park. Wildflowers to watch for include the spectacular rose pogonia, spider lily, green fly orchid and the carnivorous trumpet pitcher-plant. Don't forget the mansion, a center of political, social and commercial activity since its construction more than 250 years ago. Washington, Lafayette and Francis Marion visited, and you should, too!

When to go: The park is open Thursday through Monday, from 9 a.m. to 6 p.m., with the mansion open from 1 p.m. until 4 p.m.

How to get there: From McClellanville, drive about 7.0 miles north on US 17. Turn left onto Rutledge Road at the state park sign and drive about 2.5 miles to the park entrance.

Extras: There is a fee to enter the mansion. Appointments suggested for groups. Call (843) 546-9361 for information about the park.

77 Cape Romain National Wildlife Refuge

A boat ride through the 64,000-acre refuge from Moore's Landing to Bulls Island takes you through coastal marshes and open water to an undeveloped barrier island. Sixteen miles of hiking trails on the island cross maritime forests, freshwater impoundments (remnants of the island's hunting retreat past) and pristine beaches.

What to look for: Begin at the Sewee Visitor and Environmental Education Center, then drive to Moore's Landing. While you can see salt marshes, wading birds and shorebirds from the landing, you can't really appreciate all this refuge has to offer without boating to Bulls or one of the smaller islands in the refuge. Watch for bottlenosed dolphins and for shorebirds like black skimmers and oystercatchers. On the island, look for songbirds — warblers, vireos, tanagers, thrushes and others — as well as wild turkeys, quail, deer and bobcats. Wood ducks, green-winged teal and other waterfowl occupy inland ponds, along with large alligators and turtles. You may see eagles, hawks and other birds of prey. Hurricane Hugo devastated the islands in 1989, changing the habitat dramatically. One positive change is an increase in sunny patches ideal for wildflowers and butterflies. Bulls Island houses reproducing red wolves, an endangered species that became extinct in the wild in the mid-1970s. You probably won't see these secretive animals on the island, but you <u>can</u> see them at the Sewee Center.

When to go: The best times to visit are spring and fall. Sewee Visitor and Environmental Center is open from 9 a.m to 5 p.m Tuesday through Sunday and is closed on major holidays.

How to get there: Sewee Center is on US 17 at Awendaw, about 20 miles northeast of Charleston. The ramp at Moore's Landing (open during daylight hours, best at high tide) is available to the public.

Extras: Call (843) 928-3368 for information. A private ferry service takes visitors to Bulls Island on Saturdays during December through February, and Tuesdays, Thursdays, Fridays and Saturdays during the remainder of the year. Call (843) 881-4582 to arrange a trip. Plan carefully, as water and restrooms are available in only one location on Bulls Island.

It appears this royal tern (Sterna maxima) *would like to have a few words with the photographer.*
Photo by Ted Borg.

Very common all along the east coast, sand dollars (Mellita isometra) *are closely related to sea urchins. There are different species, distinguished primarily by the number of oval openings present.* Photo by Robert Clark.

If you want to experience an undisturbed coastal barrier island and you have a boat, this is the place to go. Only one island separates Capers from the heavily developed Isle of Palms, yet the two are worlds apart.

What to look for: Most, if not all, of the wading birds and shorebirds that occur in South Carolina can be found in the 2,000 acres of maritime forest, beaches and salt marsh of Capers Island Heritage Preserve. Watch for American oystercatchers and willets in the marshes. Eagles and ospreys are likely to soar overhead, joined in the fall by other birds of prey. Watch the sea for loons and sea ducks in the winter. Loggerhead sea turtles and manatees are occasionally seen in the summer. Dolphins are likely to pass by at any time. In the upland areas, more than 75 species of songbirds have been sighted. Lucky observers may catch sight of a bobcat, mink or river otter . . . or at least their tracks! Watch for diamondback terrapins and snapping turtles, too. Alligators, of course, are common.

When to go: Low tide during the spring and fall is the best time to observe birds.

How to get there: Capers Island is north of Dewees Island and south of Bull Island in the Cape Romain National Wildlife Refuge. Nearby public boat landings include Moore's Landing (available during daylight hours at high tide) on the Intracoastal Waterway and the Gadsonville Landing (available at high tide only) on Copahee Sound (behind Dewees Island.) Navigational charts are recommended, as tidal creeks may be confusing.

Extras: For information about the preserve, call (843) 762-5062. Beachfront primitive camping allowed with free permit obtained by calling DNR at (843) 762-5062. Boats may use Capers Island dock to unload, but should be anchored away from the dock.

79 Fort Johnson - Marine Resources Center

The brown pelican (Pelecanus occidentalis) *can glide with its wingtips just above the water or make a spectacular, head-first dive in pursuit of a meal. The bill's pouch separates the catch from water. Photo by Ted Borg.*

Perched on the southern edge of Charleston Harbor, Fort Johnson is a great place to see wading birds, shorebirds, migrating songbirds and raptors, even though scores of people flock there to work at the DNR's Marine Center each day. The Center is one of the largest and most sophisticated marine research and management facilities on the East Coast. During business hours, the main laboratory building's lobby is open to the public and contains several displays about programs and projects underway at the Center, as well as a display about the history of Fort Johnson.

What to look for: At low tide, wading birds patrol the mud flats around the Marine Resources Center hoping to find a meal. Four species of tern frequent Fort Johnson in the summer. Summer also brings brown pelicans flying low over the water. In the winter, less-common shorebird species such as American oystercatchers and black-bellied plovers also can be seen here, joining waterfowl including red-breasted mergansers, greater scaup, red-throated loons, common loons and common goldeneyes. During fall migrations, watch for birds of prey, including bald eagles and peregrine falcons. More than 100 resident and coastal migrant songbird species pass through. In the harbor, look for dolphins and an occasional manatee.

When to go: The Marine Center gate is open from about 7 a.m. to 6 p.m. Monday through Friday, but the area can be entered on foot any time during daylight hours. Best viewing is at low tide in spring and fall. Winter is the best time to see waterfowl and shorebirds.

How to get there: From Charleston, take SC 30 south 2 miles to the Harborview Road exit. Turn right and go about 2 miles to the end of the road. At the stop sign, turn left onto Ft. Johnson Road, which will end at the facility gate.

Extras: Interpretive displays and library (on-site use only) available in main lab building. For more information, call (843) 795-6350.

The Ashepoo, Combahee and Edisto (ACE) rivers flow lazily through cypress swamps, old rice fields and tidal marshes before emptying into St. Helena Sound. Together, they mark the boundaries of one of the largest undeveloped wetland ecosystems remaining on the Atlantic coast. The area was once a center of plantation rice culture in South Carolina; later, wealthy sportsmen purchased old plantations to use as hunting retreats. The land became an undeveloped, unpolluted haven for wildlife, and much of it remains so today because of the ACE Basin Project, a joint protection effort by federal, state and private organizations in cooperation with private land-owners. The goal of the project is to protect 200,000 acres of

diverse wetland and upland habitats within the 350,000 acres of the basin. The ACE Basin Project has become a model for other parts of the country, and for similar efforts in other "focus areas" of South Carolina. Walterboro, the Colleton County seat, is the starting point for any trip by land into the ACE Basin. The ACE Basin National Estuarine Research Reserve, Bear Island WMA, ACE Basin National Wildlife Refuge and Donnelley WMA are all part of the ACE Basin Area. For information about lodging or other local attractions, contact the Walterboro/Colleton Chamber of Commerce at (843) 549-9595.

Top: *The St. Helena Sound is formed at the confluence of the Ashepoo, Edisto and Combahee rivers.* Photo by Phillip Jones. Above: *Designed by colonists and virtually unchanged in 300 years, rice trunks are utilized in present times to manipulate water levels in managed wetlands.* Photo by Ted Borg.

81 Edisto River

Reportedly the world's longest free-flowing blackwater river, the Edisto begins in the midlands of the state and ends at the Atlantic Ocean. Blackwater rivers are so named because of the color added by tannins in the vegetation surrounding the river. The same vegetation that colors the river also creates beautiful green walls along its edge, best appreciated from a canoe or other small boat.

What to look for: Besides beautiful scenery, the Edisto is known for its redbreast sunfish (license required to catch them!), which nest in gravel shoals near the banks. Deer, foxes, river otters and alligators may watch you from the bank, while wading birds, ducks and belted kingfishers will join you in the river. Wildflowers, along with butterflies and humming-birds, are common along the banks in spring and fall. Huge live oaks draped in Spanish moss add both shade and an air of mystery to the river.

When to go: If you plan to reach the river from one of the state parks, your visit will be limited by their hours of operation (9 a.m. until 6 p.m. November through March, 9 a.m. until 9 p.m. April through October.) Public boat landings are always open.

How to get there: You can reach the river from Colleton State Park, Givhans Ferry State Park, or one of 10 public boat landings. From Exit 68 on I-95 in Colleton County, take SC 61 East to reach either park. See county maps for public boat ramp locations.

Extras: Both parks offer camping and fishing. Call (843) 538-8206 (Colleton) or (843) 873-0692 (Givhans Ferry) for information. Guided trips on the river are available. Call (843) 549-9595 for information.

The Edisto River Canoe and Kayak Trail affords paddlers 56 miles of blackwater nature viewing.
Photo by Ted Borg.

Take a long or short walk on Westvaco's Edisto Nature Trail that meanders through a typical Lowcountry forest. Along the way, watch for evidence of how the land was used in former days: canals, the historic King's Highway, old rice fields, and an abandoned phosphate plant site.

What to look for: Most of the one-mile "long trail" follows an old railroad tram right-of-way through a cypress swamp. These trams were used to haul lumber or crops to the nearest railroad line, and many of the raised rights-of-way still criss-cross the Lowcountry. Watch for raccoons, wood ducks, deer and other species common to lowland swamps. Many migrating songbirds pass through the area, joining a variety of resident species. Look for wood thrushes, warblers and woodpeckers. Birds of prey such as hawks and owls are present year-round. In spring, watch for the beautiful atamasco lilies springing up in damp ground. This is a

The graceful fronds of dwarf palmetto (Sabal minor) *are common along the trail.* Photo by Phillip Jones.

good spot to look for salamand ers and lizards. The half-mile "short trail" provides a perfect opportunity for families with young children to learn about forest ecology firsthand — without wearing out short legs. The Pon Pon spur trail leads through a bottomland hardwood swamp to the Edisto River. ("Pon Pon" is the name of the Native American village that once stood on the site of historic Jacksonboro.)

When to go: The trail is open seven days a week. Best viewing will be in the spring and fall, and more birds will be spotted early in the morning. After very wet weather, the long trail may be closed because of flooding.

How to get there: The trail is located on US 17 in Jacksonboro, southeast of the Colleton County seat of Walterboro. As you travel north, the parking lot and entrance will be on the left, shortly after the intersection of US 17 and SC 64.

Extras: Trail guides provided by Westvaco in the black mailbox next to the map at the beginning of the trail. Call (843) 871-5000 for information about group presentations. Outdoor amphitheater available.

83 ACE Basin National Wildlife Refuge

The two units of the National Wildlife Refuge offer visitors a sampling of habitats ranging from upland forests to tidal marsh. The refuge also offers a glimpse into the cultural history of the ACE Basin. Refuge headquarters is The Grove Plantation House, built in 1828 and one of only three area antebellum homes to survive the Civil War.

<u>What to look for:</u> Almost half the land in the NWR is salt marsh, one of nature's most productive ecosystems. As the tides recede, look for crabs and other crustaceans scurrying in the mud. You won't be the only one looking — wading birds and shorebirds will be searching for their next meal. If you're lucky, you'll see wood storks, as well as herons, ibises and other wading birds. Look for migrating songbirds, including painted and indigo buntings, blue grosbeaks and summer tanagers. Bald eagles and an occasional peregrine falcon may pass overhead.

<u>When to go:</u> The refuge is open from dawn to dark, seven days a week. Some impoundments and nesting areas will be closed from time to time to protect sensitive species. During deer hunts, the upland areas will be closed to those not hunting. Call the refuge to ensure availability.

<u>How to get there:</u> From Jacksonboro, in Colleton County, drive about 6 miles north on US 17, to the intersection with SC 174. Follow SC 174 to Adams Run and turn right at the flashing light onto Willtown Road. The refuge entrance road is 2 miles from this intersection.

<u>Extras:</u> You can fish in the tidal creeks and streams. For information call (843) 889-3084.

*Thick, mysterious Spanish moss (*Tillandsia usneoides*) and a long-forgotten fishing pier combine for quaint scenery.*
Photo by Phillip Jones.

If you have only a short while to spend in the Lowcountry, you should spend some time here. The 8,048-acre Donnelley WMA harbors some of every Lowcountry habitat type, except coastal beaches, and good nature viewing is guaranteed.

<u>What to look for:</u> Old rice fields and other wetlands host a variety of water-fowl and wading birds. This is a good place to look for the wood stork,

Ten inches long when hatched, alligators (Alligator mississippiensis) *grow into the largest reptiles on our continent, reaching lengths of over 15 feet.* Photo by Ted Borg.

the only stork native to the United States. Watch for a range of shore birds, including plovers and rarely seen avocets. In the uplands, look for songbirds such as warblers and buntings, and game species such as wild turkeys, doves and quail. You may see eagles and other birds of prey. Resident mammals include river otters and bobcats. You may surprise an alligator sunning on the road and should see many other, less obvious reptiles and amphibians. Trails cross extensive forested and tidal wetlands, agricultural lands and upland forests. The Boynton Nature Trail begins about 2 miles down the main road of the WMA. Turn right at the green Nature Trail sign. This 2.2-mile trail is an easy walk and will give you a feel for the variety of habitats on the site if your time is limited. Shortly before the trail reaches the first impoundment, a smaller trail turns right and leads to an 80-acre swamp, which provides the perfect habitat for nesting wood ducks.

<u>When to go:</u> Donnelley WMA is open Monday through Saturday from 8 a.m. until 5 p.m. Except for one designated trail, the area is closed Sundays and during scheduled hunts. Please call ahead to ensure availability. Trails in and around the managed wetland complex are closed from November 1 through January 20 to reduce disturbance to waterfowl. The best water-fowl viewing opportunities are from late January through mid-March.

<u>How to get there:</u> The entrance is immediately north of the intersection of US 17 and SC 303 near Green Pond.

<u>Extras:</u> Register at the entrance kiosk near the office before entering. Group tours available. Call (843) 844-8957 for information.

85 Bear Island Wildlife Management Area

Expect to see broad expanses of marsh at Bear Island WMA, as well as upland forests and rice fields managed much as they were in antebellum days, except that today's "crop" is wildlife.

A pintail hen and drake (Anas acuta) *float on the flooded remains of an old rice field.*
Photo by Robert Clark.

What to look for: In late winter and early spring, ducks rise in clouds from the old rice fields. As the spring progresses, they're replaced by wading birds and shore birds. Watch for ibises, avocets and black-necked stilts. The site also boasts an eagle's nest within sight of the picnic area. Spring and fall are the best times to look for migrating songbirds. You won't have to work to see alligators, but other reptiles and amphibians may be more elusive. The 12,021-acre site also conceals a selection of hard-to-find plants, including carnivorous pitcher-plants and orchids.

When to go: The WMA is open for general public use during daylight hours, Monday through Saturday from January 21 through October 31. From November 1 to January 20, visitors can only view the impoundments from Bennett's Point Road (SC 26), the entrance gate at WMA head-quarters, or the observation deck on SC 26 just north of the WMA entrance. Best viewing times are mornings and late afternoons in the spring and fall.

How to get there: From Green Pond, drive about 3 miles north on US 17 to S-15-26 (Bennett's Point Road). Turn right on S-15-26 and drive about 13 miles. The observation deck will be on the right, and the main entrance will be approximately 1,000 feet farther on the left.

Extras: Sign in at the entrance kiosk. Safety considerations preclude private vehicles on most dikes, but bicycles are allowed. (Wide tires work best!) Watch for alligators and venomous snakes. Tours or presentations can be arranged. Call (843) 844-8957 for information.

If you have access to a boat, the ACE Basin NERR is one of the best places to appreciate the full extent of the basin and its resources. From the two coastal state parks (Edisto Beach and Hunting Island) that guard the entrance, to the interior tidal marshes, the NERR captures the magnificence of "the salty side" of the ACE Basin.

<u>What to look for:</u> Watch for threatened loggerhead sea turtles, bottlenosed dolphins and the occasional manatee as you cruise the 12,000 acres of estuarine waters. The area is rich in saltwater and estuarine fish, shellfish and crustaceans. Birds of all types will surround you: ducks, wading birds, shorebirds and sea birds such as terns and pelicans. More than 50 species of songbirds also call the basin home. On or near the half-dozen small wooded islands, look for diamondback terrapins, island glass lizards, and mammals such as river otters, mink, bobcats and marsh rabbits. Otter, Ashe, Beet and Warren islands are all within St. Helena Sound and all are Heritage Preserves where various restrictions on activity may apply.

<u>When to go:</u> Best viewing times are at low tide in fall, winter and spring.

<u>How to get there:</u> From Jacksonboro, drive 6.5 miles south on US 17. Turn left on S-15-26 (Bennett's Point Road) and drive about 18 miles to the end of the paved road and turn right. A public boat ramp and the NERR Field Station are about 100 yards on the left.

<u>Extras:</u> Navigational charts ***strongly recommended.*** Coastal Adventure Cruise Program for high school and college student groups and other educational programs available. Call (843) 762-5437 for information about the NERR. Call (803) 734-3983 for information about specific Heritage Preserves or about the state's Heritage Trust Program.

*South Carolina's population of raccoons (*Procyon lotor*) is densest along the coast, where the ringtails feed on crayfish, clams, fruits and berries.*
Photo by Ted Borg.

87 Edisto Beach State Park

Edisto Beach is famous for the fossilized teeth of sharks, bison and mammals now extinct that seem to be more common here than elsewhere. More recent history is reflected in the shell mounds and other legacies of Native American inhabitants of the land encompassed by the 1,225-acre park.

<u>What to look for:</u> Edisto Beach State Park boasts some of the tallest palmetto trees in the state. Beachcombers love the 1.5 miles of ocean beach, where typical Southeastern marine life is found. Watch for bottlenosed dolphins offshore. Make time to visit the salt marshes on the upland side of the park as well. The 4-mile Spanish Mount Trail makes it easy to explore the maritime forest and marshes. Migrant songbirds are plentiful here. Be on the lookout for painted buntings in dense shrub thickets. Watch for evidence of bobcats — they're here, and if you're up early you may catch sight of one. In the summer, loggerhead turtles come ashore to lay their eggs. *It is against state and federal laws to disturb turtles, nests or hatchlings.*

<u>When to go:</u> The park is open from 6 a.m. until 10 p.m. April through October and from 8 a.m. until 6 p.m. during the remainder of the year.

<u>How to get there:</u> From US 17, take SC 174 to the park.

<u>Extras:</u> Park has 5 cabins, beachfront and marsh-view campsites and a gift shop/store. Interpretive programs available on a seasonal basis; check schedule at the park entrance. Parking fee charged. Boat ramp available. Call (843) 869-2156 for camping information. For general information, call (843) 869-2756.

Left: *Wide, unspoiled beaches and towering palmettos* (Sabal palmetto) *are among the most distinctive features at the park.*
Photo by Michael Foster.
Inset: *Sections of the beach are heaped with blue, gray, white and pink oyster shells.*
Photo by Phillip Jones.

As the name implies, this park is an island — a beautiful 5,000-acre semi-tropical barrier island. Within its boundaries are one of the few remaining 19th-century lighthouses in the Southeast, sandy beaches, a fishing pier, and trails and boardwalks traversing marsh and maritime forest.

Sea oats (Uniola paniculata) *and palmettos* (Sabal palmetto) *frame the Hunting Island Lighthouse. Listed on the National Register of Historic Places, it's the only lighthouse in South Carolina open to the public.* Photo by Phillip Jones.

What to look for: Visit the lighthouse for an excellent view of the coastline. The 0.5-mile Lighthouse Nature Trail crosses maritime forest, skirts the edge of a freshwater marsh and ends on the beach. Look for wading birds and songbirds such as painted buntings, orchard orioles and summer tanagers. On the 0.3-mile marsh boardwalk, you'll see more wading birds, and at low tide, the footprints of mammals like raccoons, otters and mink. Near the Visitor Center, a short boardwalk leads over a pond to an observation deck, the best place to view alligators. On the beach, watch the surf for bottlenosed dolphins and the sky for marine birds, including the black skimmer and laughing gull. Threatened loggerhead sea turtles nest on the beaches in summer, generally in June. The park implements a lights out policy on summer nights to protect the nesting turtles. ***It is against state and federal laws to disturb turtles, hatchlings, or marker flags.***

When to go: The park is open from 6 a.m. to 9 p.m. April through October and 6 a.m. to 6 p.m. November through March. The Interpretive Center is open from 9 a.m. to 5 p.m. Monday through Friday and 11 a.m. until 5 p.m. on weekends. Best alligator watching is during the summer, while spring and fall are the best nature viewing times on the Lighthouse Trail and Marsh Boardwalk.

How to get there: Travel 16 miles east of Beaufort on US 21. The park is accessible by bridge.

Extras: Park has 200 campsites, 15 fully supplied cabins and a park store. Guided sea turtle walks and other special programs frequently available; call (843) 838-2011 for information. Ocean swimming, crabbing, and surf, pier and lagoon fishing available. Parking fee charged.

89 Webb Wildlife Management Area

Once owned by the Belmont family of horse-racing fame, this property now offers a multitude of opportunities to see a diverse array of habitat types and wildlife species. Hunters and anglers have long known it as a recreational mecca, but wildlife watchers are beginning to discover it, too.

This white-tail buck (Odocoileus virginianus) *is "in velvet;" his antlers are covered with a soft skin. Note turkeys* (Meleagris gallopavo) *in background.*
Photo by Art Carter.

What to look for: The property is intensively managed for game species like deer, quail and turkeys, and ponds are stocked with bass, bluegill and shellcracker. Endangered red-cockaded woodpeckers prefer the same conditions as quail and are found in the upland areas of the center. More than 2,300 acres of bottom-land hardwood forest lie within the center's boundaries, fed by the wide Savannah River flood plain. Both a 1-mile canoe trail and a 2-mile walking trail lead through the swamp. Hidden within the flood plain is Bluff Lake, once a part of the Savannah River and now filled with tall cypress trees. Listen for the call of the bird-voiced treefrog. In South Carolina, it's found only in the swamps of the Savannah River and its tributaries south of Aiken. Other uncommon species seen here include swallow-tailed and Mississippi kites. Watch for migrating songbirds, including buntings and a variety of warblers.

When to go: The best viewing times are January, February, March and May. The Webb Center is open during daylight hours year-round except for the months of April, September, October, November and December, when it is closed to general visitation during scheduled hunts.

How to get there: From Estill, take US 321 south 10 miles to Garnett. Bear right on SC 119, drive about 60 yards and turn right again on S-25-20 (Augusta Stagecoach Road). Cross the railroad tracks and drive 2.4 miles to the Webb Center entrance on the left. Follow the dirt road 1.4 miles to the office on the right.

Extras: All visitors must check in at the office. Boat access available at Stokes Bluff boat landing. Organized groups may arrange extended programs or tours by prior appointment. The lodge and meeting facility are available on a limited basis to approved nature-oriented groups. Standard fees charged for overnight lodging and meals. For information, call (803) 625-3569.

In South Carolina, **gopher tortoises** are only found in small areas of Jasper, Hampton and Aiken counties. This 953-acre preserve permanently protects one of their few known habitats.

What to look for: Gopher tortoises (called "gophers") are a state endangered species inhabiting sandy areas covered in longleaf pine, turkey oak and

The Eastern diamondback rattlesnake (Crotalus adamanteus) is the largest rattler in the United States. It sometimes uses tortoise burrows as its home; give this animal a wide berth. Photo by Ted Borg.

wiregrass. Tillman Sand Ridge provides ideal conditions for the tortoises, and their burrows, which may be as long as 10 meters, in turn provide ideal conditions for up to 360 other animal species. Some of these species are uncommon, such as the crawfish frog, or dangerous, such as the Eastern diamondback rattlesnake. *Do not disturb the tortoises or their burrows.* Because the preserve extends from cypress and bottomland hardwood swamps to sandhills, a variety of birds have been seen within its borders. Look for prothonotary warblers, painted and indigo buntings, pileated woodpeckers, loggerhead shrikes and large birds of prey. Red-tailed, red-shouldered, Cooper's and sharp-shinned hawks, barred, great-horned and screech owls, and kestrels all inhabit the site. It is also a great spot to see butterflies, including less common species like the zebra swallowtail. Invading armadillos, which are extending their range slowly northward, are also found on the site.

When to go: The best viewing time is spring, when the tortoises emerge from their burrows. The preserve is open for hiking and bird-watching throughout the year, but visitors should be aware of hunting seasons.

How to get there: The preserve is 5 miles west of Tillman on S-27-119. Park at the second gate, adjacent to the preserve's information sign. To reach the B & C public boat landing on the southern border of the preserve, bear left on S-27-201 and follow the road until it ends at the landing.

Extras: Walk the trails or travel by 4WD vehicle unless roads are closed by gates or signs. Be careful on sandy roads. For information about this preserve or the state's Heritage Trust Program, call (803) 734-3893.

91 Savannah National Wildlife Refuge

Because the refuge is located at the southernmost point in the state, it attracts species not likely to be seen elsewhere. The Savannah port facilities visible in the distance don't seem to bother the large numbers of waterfowl and wading birds that come to rest on the freshwater impoundments of the refuge; neither do they bother the many migrating songbirds that stop here to visit.

<u>What to look for:</u> Within the 26,000 acres of marshes, bottomland hardwood swamps and creeks stretching along both sides of the Savannah River are 3,000 acres of former rice fields. Trails and roads along these impoundments allow even those with limited mobility to see a wide variety of coastal wildlife. The refuge is used heavily by wintering waterfowl, and wading and shorebirds are always abundant. The bird list for the refuge includes close to 300 species, some of which, like the wood stork, peregrine falcon, bald eagle and swallow-tailed kite, are endangered or of special concern. Others, like the gaudy purple gallinule, are simply fun to watch. The Cistern Trail, a short walking trail leading from the Laurel Hill Wildlife Drive, is an excellent place to see warblers and other migrants. On rare occasions, manatees are seen in the tidal waters during warmer months.

Flying close to the ground, Northern harriers (Circus cyaneus) *take their prey by surprise. They are thought to rely more on keen hearing than sight.* Photo by Ted Borg.

<u>When to go:</u> The Laurel Hill Wildlife Drive and most walking trails are open to the public year-round during daylight hours. From December 1 to February 28, the impounded area north of US 17 is closed to reduce disturbance to wintering waterfowl. The best viewing opportunities are between October and April, with the largest concentrations of waterfowl between November and February.

<u>How to get there:</u> To reach the Laurel Hill Wildlife Drive from Hardeeville, travel south on US 17 for 5 miles, then to SC 170 for 1 mile. Follow signs to the refuge entrance.

<u>Extras:</u> Fishing permitted in freshwater pools from March 1 to November 30. Restrooms available at the entrance to Laurel Hill Wildlife Drive only. For more information, call (912) 652-4415.

Tucked into the rapidly growing Hilton Head/Bluffton area, this preserve ensures that more than 1,000 acres of habitat along the Colleton River will remain undisturbed. It also shelters one of the best-known populations of the rare plant pondspice in the U.S.

<u>What to look for:</u> Victoria Bluff is an excellent example of the once-common pine/saw palmetto community that depends on periodic burning to maintain its health. Many wet depressions ranging in size from 0.1 acre to 10 acres provide the habitat essential for pondspice. The inland maritime forest, consisting of palmettos, live oaks and other hardwoods, is also an interesting habitat. In the pines, look for brown-headed nuthatches and pine warblers. Hooded and yellow-throated warblers, wood thrushes, white-eyed vireos, great crested flycatchers and summer tanagers also frequent the property. Look for mole salamanders in the wet areas and for the beautiful (and non-venomous) scarlet kingsnake. The many firebreaks across the property provide excellent access for hiking, horseback riding and nature study.

<u>When to go:</u> The preserve is open at all times. Hunting is allowed, therefore, if you are in the woods during hunting season, be sure to wear brightly colored clothing.

<u>How to get there:</u> From the bridge joining Hilton Head to the mainland, travel west on US 278 for 2 miles. Turn right on Sawmill Creek Road, following signs for the Waddell Mariculture Center. The preserve begins at US 278 and extends toward the Colleton River. Park on any of the side roads.

<u>Extras:</u> The Waddell Mariculture Center, operated by the S.C. DNR, is close to the end of the road leading through the preserve. Call (843) 837-3795 for information. Public boat landing offers a beautiful view of the Colleton River and a good spot to fish at the end of the road. Area may harbor ticks, cottonmouths and copperheads — stay alert. For information about the preserve or the state's Heritage Trust Program, call (803) 734-3893.

The female marbled salamander (Ambystoma opacum) *lays 50-200 eggs in a depression on dry land. Larvae hatch a few days after rain fills the depression; they take adult form in about five months. Photo by Ted Borg.*

93 Pinckney Island National Wildlife Refuge

Once the plantation home of Revolutionary War commander, candidate for president and signer of the U.S. Constitution Charles Cotesworth Pinckney, the island now provides a sheltered refuge for wading birds, shorebirds, waterfowl and a host of other animals.

What to look for: The 14 miles of grass and gravel nature trails make it easy to explore the many habitats on Pinckney, the largest island within the 4,053-acre refuge and the only one on which public use is allowed. Trails pass through maritime forest, salt marsh and open fields and near five freshwater ponds. "Osprey" and "Ibis" ponds are the most accessible. Because they provide valuable fresh water, they're a magnet for wildlife. Look for turtles, snakes, fish and frogs, which feed larger pond residents. Snowy and cattle egrets, tri-colored, night and little blue herons have all nested at Osprey and Ibis ponds, which may be closed during certain seasons to protect the wildlife. During the fall and winter, the refuge's fresh and salt waters attract ducks; more than 19 species have been recorded. You're likely to see endangered wood storks, along with ibises, willets, sandpipers and oystercatchers. Watch the mud flats for footprints of raccoons, otters and deer, all of which make a home here.

When to go: The refuge is open daily during daylight hours. More migrating songbirds will be seen in spring and fall, while more waterfowl will be drawn to the refuge's freshwater ponds and surrounding salt water in fall and winter. As in any tidal area, wildlife will be more evident as the tide recedes, allowing birds and mammals to feed on snails, fiddler crabs and other small animals in the exposed mud flats.

How to get there: The entrance to the refuge is on US 278, 0.5 mile west of Hilton Head Island. Look for the sign between Mackay and Skull creeks as you cross the bridge.

Extras: Public boat ramp provides excellent access to Intracoastal Waterway (Skull Creek) at Last End Point. Bicycles are a great way to tour the refuge. Call (912) 652-4415 for information.

Freshwater ponds and a rich variety of vegetation draw wildlife onto the refuge in remarkable numbers. Photo by Phillip Jones.

Nature viewing areas featured in this guide are provided by government agencies, corporations and private individuals for public visitation. The landowners listed below have graciously volunteered to include their areas in the Nature Viewing Program. Visitors are asked to respect the regulations that apply to each area, collect litter, and avoid disturbing plants and animals on the property. Such respect will ensure the continued participation of these landowners in the Nature Viewing Program.

Abbreviations used in this guide:

DNR	SC Department of Natural Resources
FS	Forest Service
FWS	Fish and Wildlife Service
HP	Heritage Preserve
NF	National Forest
NWR	National Wildlife Refuge
PRT	SC Department of Parks, Recreation & Tourism
PSA	SC Public Service Authority
Rv	River
SP	State Park
WMA	Wildlife Management Area

MOUNTAINS

1. Chattooga River: USDA FS
2. Buzzards Roost HP: DNR
3. Sumter National Forest - Andrew Pickens District: USDA FS
4. Oconee SP: PRT
5. Walhalla State Fish Hatchery: DNR
6. Foothills Trail: USDA FS, PRT, Duke Energy
7. Bad Creek/Lower Whitewater River: Duke Energy
8. Devils Fork SP: PRT
9. Keowee-Toxaway SP: PRT
10. Jocassee Gorges/Laurel Fork HP: DNR
11. Eastatoe Creek HP: DNR
12. Table Rock SP: PRT
13. Mountain Bridge Wilderness & Recreation Area: PRT, DNR
14. Glassy Mountain HP: DNR
15. Bunched Arrowhead HP: DNR
16. Paris Mountain SP: PRT

PIEDMONT

17. SC Botanical Gardens: Clemson University
18. Fant's Grove Wildlife Demonstration Area: Clemson University
19. John de la Howe School Interpretive Trail: State of South Carolina
20. Savannah District Lakes: U.S.Army Corps of Engineers
21. Stevens Creek HP: DNR
22. Sumter National Forest - Long Cane District: USDA FS
23. Pacolet River HP: DNR
24. Chester County Turkey Management Demonstration Area: Bowater
25. Union County Turkey Management Demonstration Area: Bowater
26. Rose Hill Plantation SP: PRT
27. Sumter National Forest - Enoree Ranger District: USDA FS
28. Lake Monticello/Parr Reservoir/Broad River Waterfowl Management Area: SC Electric & Gas Co.

29. Kings Mountain SP: PRT
30. Rock Hill Blackjacks HP: DNR
31. Landsford Canal SP: PRT
32. Flat Creek/Forty-Acre Rock HP: DNR
33. Lake Wateree Dam/Lugoff Access Area: Duke Energy

SANDHILLS

34. Savannah River Bluffs HP: DNR
35. Hitchcock Woods: The Hitchcock Foundation
36. Aiken SP: PRT
37. Aiken Gopher Tortoise HP: DNR
38. Harbison State Forest: SC Forestry Commission
39. Native Habitat Learning Center/ Clemson University Sandhill Research & Education Center: Clemson University
40. Carolina Sandhills NWR: USDI FWS
41. Sand Hills State Forest/Sugarloaf Mountain: SC Forestry Commission
42. Cheraw Fish Hatchery: DNR
43. Cheraw SP: PRT

COASTAL PLAIN

44. Poinsett SP: PRT
45. Manchester State Forest: SC Forestry Commission
46. Congaree Swamp National Monument: USDI National Park Service
47. Upper Santee Swamp of Lake Marion: Santee Cooper, SC PSA
48. Santee SP: PRT
49. Santee NWR: USDI FWS
50. Santee Cooper WMA: Santee Cooper, PSA
51. Bird Island (Lake Marion): Santee Cooper, PSA
52. Sandy Beach WMA: Santee Cooper, SC PSA
53. St. Stephen Fish Lift: US Army Corps of Engineers; Jack Bayless Hatchery: DNR
54. Lake Moultrie Passage/Palmetto Trail: Santee Cooper, PSA
55. Wadboo Creek: Santee Cooper, PSA
56. Old Santee Canal SP: PRT
57. Hatchery WMA: Santee Cooper, PSA
58. Francis Marion National Forest: USDA FS
59. Francis Beidler Forest: National Audubon Society
60. Kalmia Gardens: Coker College Segars McKinnon HP: DNR
61. Lee SP: PRT
62. Lynchburg Savanna HP: DNR
63. Woods Bay SP: PRT
64. Lynches Scenic River: N/A
65. Great Pee Dee HP & WMA: DNR
66. Little Pee Dee HP & WMA: DNR
67. Cartwheel Bay HP & WMA: DNR
68. Lewis Ocean Bay HP & WMA: DNR
69. Waccamaw River HP & WMA: DNR
70. Myrtle Beach SP: PRT
71. Huntington Beach SP: PRT
72. Samworth WMA: DNR continued on page 112

111

Photo by Phillip Jones.

Landowners' List continued from page 111.
73. Tom Yawkey Wildlife Center: DNR
74. Santee Coastal Reserve WMA: DNR
75. Santee Delta WMA: DNR
76. Hampton Plantation SP: PRT
77. Cape Romain NWR: USDI FWS
78. Capers Island HP: DNR
79. Fort Johnson -
    Marine Resources Center: DNR
80. ACE Basin: Cooperative ownership
    among private individuals,
    conservation organizations, and
    state and federal agencies.
81. Edisto River: N/A

82. Edisto Nature Trail: Westvaco
83. ACE Basin NWR: USDI FWS
84. Donnelly WMA: U.S.Army Corps of
    Engineers; DNR; Ducks Unlimited
85. Bear Island WMA: DNR
86. ACE Basin National Estuarine
    Research Reserve: DNR
87. Edisto Beach SP: PRT
88. Hunting Island SP: PRT
89. Webb WMA: DNR
90. Tillman Sand Ridge HP & WMA: DNR
91. Savannah NWR: USDI FWS
92. Victoria Bluff HP & WMA: DNR
93. Pinckney Island NWR: USDI FWS

Reduce, Reuse,
Recycle.
Help keep
South Carolina
green!

Remember,
only you can
prevent
forest fires.

Lend a hand!
Care for the land!

for wildlife
for the land
for the water
for others
for South Carolina